The Re-Emergence of the Divine Feminine and its Significance for Spiritual, Psychological and Evolutionary Growth

Franceska Perot

Boca Raton

The Re-Emergence of the Divine Feminine and its Significance
for Spiritual, Psychological and Evolutionary Growth

Dissertation.com
Boca Raton, Florida
USA • 2008

ISBN-10: 1-58112- 390-6
ISBN-13: 978-1-58112-390-6

WESTBROOK UNIVERSITY

**The Re-Emergence of the Divine Feminine and its Significance
for Spiritual, Psychological and Evolutionary Growth**

A DISSERTATION SUBMITTED TO
THE FACULTY OF TRANSPERSONAL PSYCHOLOGY
IN CANDIDACY FOR THE DEGREE OF
DOCTOR OF PHILOSOPHY

SCHOOL OF PSYCHOLOGY
COLLEGE OF HUMANITIES

BY
FRANCESKA PEROT

TOMBALL, TEXAS
SEPTEMBER 30, 2004

To Mom – thanks for being an inspiration as an Aphrodite
Archetype and an Athena career woman.

Genesis was the beginning of the end for the goddess.

Dan Brown, The DaVinci Code

Table of Contents

Preface

I have always been very interested in Goddess archetypes and how they influence psychological, spiritual and even evolutionary growth. I have noticed a rise in their popularity in the past few decades. I had hoped at the outset of this program over four and ½ years ago that I could write a paper on Goddesses. Although I would never call myself a feminist, I definitely had some feminist leanings when I started research on this paper. I have since come to realize that it is not a contest, if the feminine side or the masculine wins, then no one wins. We must all join together to envision a new paradigm that honors both paths. This is important for the survival of our species and our planet. We cannot continue this path of destruction of nature and wars against ourselves. But also we cannot return to the idyllic Paleolithic times of the Goddess. We have grown consciously and now we must use all of our resources to insure not only our survival but also our success.

Acknowledgements

I would like to thank all those individuals who supported me along the way. It has been four and ½ years since I started this program and I am happy that it is nearing its conclusion. I have had to escape many responsibilities in order to see this program come to fruition and I thank those who took up the slack for me.

I would also like to thank my friends from work, my support group, the "Goddesses" who took my tests and participated in my studies as subjects or interested parties. Thanks for all of your assistance and patience along the way.

Franceska Perot

Summary (Abstract)

For millennia a patriarchal society has ruled to the exclusion of the feminine or the Goddess who was peacefully worshipped before being completely replaced by a warrior Father God. The Goddess and hence women have been relegated to 2nd class citizens. The concept of woman as defined by traditional patriarchal society has disempowered the female sex and deemed them inferior. This exclusion and denigration of the divine feminine has done serious damage to women and men both individually and collectively, not to mention the damage this masculine mindset has caused to the environment through wars and other aggressive acts.

In this dissertation, the history of the Goddess from the Paleolithic to the present is discussed and causes for the rise of patriarchy, such as invasions by warrior cults, the advent of language and the development of the ego are explored. Then the re-emergence of the divine feminine and its psychological, spiritual and evolutionary effects are discussed.

This negative perception of the self by women is challenged by re-imaging women after the Greek Goddess archetypes: Athena, Hera, Demeter, Artemis, Aphrodite and Persephone. The Goddess archetypes are discussed in a therapeutical context as well as other therapeutical techniques such as aspecting, visualizations and women's' groups and circles. The author proposes the re-introduction of the "Sacred Marriage", a sacred ritual performed in temples since Neolithic times and in certain sects today, as a technique for therapy. This sexual ritual along with an understanding of the history of the divine feminine will have individual, collective and evolutionary effects.

The Re-Emergence of the Divine Feminine and its Significance for Spiritual, Psychological and Evolutionary Growth

INTRODUCTION

For the last 2,000 to 4,000 years God has been depicted as masculine in gender. This is due in part to the influence of the three major religions today – Christianity, Judaism and Islam.

For as long as 20,000 years prior to that, God was seen as feminine, Goddess. She reigned supreme and was known as Isis, Astarte, Ishtar, Cybele, Demeter, Artemis, Hera, Tara, Kali and Athena. She was a wise creator and was not only a fertility symbol but had wide-ranging societal influence on both men and women.

During her reign, women could buy and sell property, have businesses and inherit land and title from their mothers. Even in patriarchal Christianity, women can explore the lost glory of Lilith, Eve and Mary. With the advent of patriarchy, women were merely the property of their fathers and husbands, who held the power of life and death over them. Women were considered inherently sinful and were to be closely controlled. It has only been in the last few decades that the idea of a Divine Feminine is once again becoming popular and can be discussed openly without fear of reprisal, at least in most of the Western world. This movement will further be recognized as necessary for balance of the masculine and feminine, to bring the world back to order.

This re-emergence is significant for the spiritual, psychological and evolutionary growth of males and females. The resacralization of the feminine will allow males to connect with their feminine side without losing their masculinity. Females can grow spiritually and psychologically with Goddess archetypes. They now have alternatives to becoming aggressive like men or staying home to have babies, as the patriarchal view would describe femininity. All of this can be accomplished without the loss of her femininity. Her power is rooted within her and these role models will bring alternatives to current paradigms.

Both males and females can grow as was meant. This direction will lead to a balance between the sexes that will allow for evolutionary growth as it was originally intended. The pendulum has swung both ways and can come to rest in the middle to create a new paradigm, a new consciousness.

This paper will explore Goddess religions around the world both ancient and current, starting in the Paleolithic Age, during the time that humans were hunter-gathers with the discovery of "Venus" figurines and through the Neolithic Age when agriculture was invented and humans gathered in villages with a Goddess temple at the center of their community. Next the Goddess was relegated to the lesser position as consort with the invasion of warrior tribes from the North during the Iron Age. Finally, patriarchy was in full swing with the rise of Judaism and its dislike of any "idols", especially those of the Goddess.

Different theories will be presented as to how and why this shift from matriarchy to patriarchy occurred. Some theorists believe that it was the influence of Northern invaders, natural disasters or perhaps event the advent of the written language, which caused a shift in brain functioning.

A Jungian analysis of the Divine Feminine archetype or Great Mother will be presented. Lastly, feminist psychology as it applies to both male and female growth and how this growth is necessary for humans to reach the next level of evolutionary consciousness, as a species will be discussed. This new evolutionary consciousness or revolution will also be discussed.

A complete section on psychotherapeutic interventions will be presented and discussion will ensue as to how these interventions can bring about balance in men and women. Theses interventions include integrating different aspects of the Goddesses into your life so an analysis of several Goddesses and what they represent will be discussed. Integration can be accomplished through creative visualization, dreamwork, art therapy, psychodrama, women's circles and chanting Divine names. Also the author proposes the re-introduction of the "Sacred Marriage" as a therapeutic technique for growth.

A correlation between this paper and the empirical study that preceded it will be discussed. Conclusions of the thoughts presented in this paper and the future that can be brought about by the revolution of the Divine feminine will be discussed at the end of this paper.

DEFINITION OF THE GODDESS

What is the Goddess, the Divine Feminine, the Great Mother? She is the embodiment of the feminine principle, a mythological character, a psychological archetype necessary for growth and a religious figure. "The Mother Goddess, wherever she is found, is an image that inspires and focuses a perception of the universe as an organic, alive and sacred whole, in which humanity, the Earth and all life on Earth participate as her children" (Baring & Cashford, 1993). The Goddess "...contains all opposites within herself, including male and female, creation and destruction. And she recognizes that life and death are of equal weight, held in balance to preserve the order of the universe" (Husain, 1997).

In the Gnostic Christian texts found in Nag Hamadi, Egypt in 1945 (Dead Sea Scrolls) is a section, which is believed to be the voice of Sophia (divine feminine wisdom) as she describes herself in a text called *Thunder, Perfect Mind*, (Kraemer, 2004):

> For I am the first and the last.
> I am the honored one and the scorned one.
> I am the whore and the holy one.
> I am the wife and the virgin.
> I am the mother and the daughter.
> I am the barren one and many are her sons.
> I am she whose wedding is great,
> and I have not taken a husband.
> I am the midwife and she who does not bear.
> I am the solace of my labor pains.
> I am the bride and the bridegroom,
> And it is my husband who begot me.
> I am the mother of my father and the
> Sister of my husband, and he is my offspring...
> Give heed to me.
> I am the one who is disgraced and the great one.

From a psychological standpoint the Goddess is an archetype that exists in the collective unconscious. She can be fragmented into lesser Goddesses, which each have particular needs and wants which exert influence over the individual (Bolen, 1984). The Great Mother is a symbolic image whose expression is found in the Goddess represented by myth and artistic creations (Neumann, 1974). A Goddess is a psychological description of a complex female character type that we intuitively recognize in ourselves, others and our culture (Woolger, 1989).

Spiritually, the worship of the Goddess included the celebration of major events in a woman's life that are not seen today. These celebrations included rituals for the onset of menstruation, childbirth and menopause (Reilly, 1995). The Goddess can bring sustenance to the transpersonal realm, to a life that is devoid of female models (Zweig, 1990). The Great Mother is immanent as opposed to the transcendent Father God (Harvey, 1995).

The Goddess was devoted to the irreverent female sexuality. Sex was seen as sacred and was vital to nature, not vulgar (Estes, 1995). The body was beautiful and nothing to be ashamed of or hidden, it was to be celebrated and enjoyed.

HISTORY OF THE GODDESS

In order to understand where humanity needs to go it is important to understand the history of the Goddess to see where humanity has been.

The Paleolithic Age Goddess appeared as early as 20,000 B.C. in the form of statues and cave drawings. These statues of the Goddess know as "Venus" figurines have been discovered from Spain to Siberia. These figures were carved in stone or bone and sometimes in ivory. They depict a round, large-breasted motherly figure. They are usually small and often pregnant.

During this time most of the glaciers that had covered Europe and Asia had melted and grasslands now appeared which supported herds of grazing animals. Homo sapiens also appeared on the scene and hunted these animals for food.

More than 130 of the Venus statues have been discovered at Paleolithic sites (Baring, 1993). Many of the statues had some sort of red pigment on them indicating a connection with blood and markings believed to connect them with a menstrual cycle and the moon cycles. Those tribes, who did not migrate with the herds, drew their Goddess figures on the cave walls where they lived.

No similar male figures have been found. It is believed that these are fertility Goddesses due to the exaggeration of the size of the breasts and stomach. Other theories of their purpose are that they are actual women, ancient pornography or teaching models to demonstrate the birth process to first time mothers. Marija Gimbutas suggested that they were "symbolic or mythic figures used to reenact seasonal and other myths" (Gimbutas, 1991).

Due to the statues's role in rituals, they can be linked to the Goddess or her representative. But more than simple fertility Goddesses these statues conveyed the mystery of birth and the female body at that time period. Since these statues were discovered at different sites all over the two continents then this image of the Divine Feminine was a universal consciousness and not a localized ideal.

Evidence of rituals and burial sites can be found in caves. The cave symbolized the womb, where life is brought forth and where it is returned for rebirth after death. Most of these sacred sites have been found 1-2 miles inside these labyrinthine cave complexes. Wall drawings inside these caves depicted animals that represented different aspects of the Goddess and her form was usually painted at the entrance to the cave. What appears to be darts or stick and line forms flying at the animals were originally thought to be weapons for hunting (male symbols) by early archeologists – a misconception furthered by academics raised in a patriarchal environment. Recently, microscopic analysis has proven that many of these are actually depictions of trees, plants, leaves and grass.

One of the early images of the Goddess was the moon. The female menstrual cycle coincided with the moon cycles and therefore became associated with the Goddess. The phases of the moon was also associated with the phases in the life of the Mother – the crescent moon or new moon was associated with a young girl or virgin, the full moon was the Mother or pregnant adult woman and the dark moon or new moon was the wise old woman or crone.

These phases demonstrated the cyclical nature of life, an endless pattern of growth death and rebirth. Darkness was not seen as the opposite of light but just another component of the Mother Goddess. Everything was a part of their relationship with her. This lunar mythology preceded solar mythology in most cultures. The Goddess was seen as the shining light in the darkness.

Many of the burial sites of the time revealed bodies were buried in the fetal position, facing East with red ochre dye sprinkled on them. This indicates a belief in the rebirth of the body after death. Some had carvings of a vulva in stone and placed in the grave, indicating the regenerative powers of the womb. Usually also were seen carvings of a snake which was associated with rebirth due to its annual shedding of skin. Another animal commonly associated with death is the bird, which was thought to guide the spirit after death.

These sacred traditions associate the powers of life and death with women and the miracle of birth incarnated in woman's body. At this time in history, the connection between sex and childbirth 10 moons later was not understood. The female was revered as the giver of life; only the female could reproduce her own kind. Man's role as a hunter was to provide and protect the women who alone bore the responsibility of childbirth and child rearing. The evolutionary model perpetuated by the current male dominated society has colored the interpretations of these early archeological finds to be seen through the paradigm as man the hunter being dominant at the time.

Since only females could perpetuate the species, the society was matrilineal; kinship was traced through the mother as she was seen as the singular parent of her family. Possessions would be passed down to the next generation through the mother. Paternity could not be established.

During the Neolithic Age, about 10,000 B.C. to 5500 B.C., the cult of the Goddess grew and became more organized into a religion, which permeated all of society. During this age, humans learned to participate with nature instead of just reaping what was offered. The Neolithic Age is differentiated from the Paleolithic Age by the development of agriculture and the domestication of animals. Seeds could now be planted that grew into grains and were made into bread and domesticated animals provided milk eggs, meat and clothing. Humans also learned to weave cloth and make pots to store food. Tribes stopped being nomadic and settled in one community to build houses, temples and villages.

The image of the Goddess also grew and expanded to include not only birth, death and regeneration of humans, but plants and animals as well. With the knowledge of agriculture, the seasons became important. The cyclical pattern of nature was discernible and so the 10 lunar month gestation of a child became even more sacred in the Neolithic. In the beginning only women made pots, clothes and played a central role in agriculture.

Statues of Goddesses continue to be made but now with more modern methods. There are striking similarities in the statues found all over Europe from this era for at this time in history there were no tribal Gods only a universally worshipped Goddess.

The advent of agriculture and the domestication of animals introduced a very prosperous time. Settlements grew into villages and towns that housed thousands of people. These settlements were usually near water, with fertile land and pastures for animals. These people seemed to enjoy peace and their arts prospered. None of these towns were fortified against attack as it did not seem necessary. It wasn't until about 4500 B.C. that the first wave of Indo-European invaders swept down out of the North.

Archeological evidence suggests that there was no superiority of females over males. The society was matrilineal and the distribution of goods was egalitarian. Women did play essential roles in religious rituals and temples. The statues of the Goddess have changed little in the Neolithic Age except for the medium utilized. They are now carved or made in clay, marble, bone and gold.

For a long time the Goddess embodied the male attributes as well as the female attributes. Around the 6th to 7th millennia B.C. figures of the God begin to differentiate from the Goddess. The male is now seen as the power that fertilizes and the female has the gestating womb. Initially the bull or some other phallic symbol depicted the God and sometimes the God was shown also as the son of the Goddess. Sometimes the God was depicted as the corn to be harvested or cut down annually and reborn again in the spring.

One of the earliest depictions of "sacred marriage" is seen in a statue of a man and woman in an embrace dated about 4500 B.C. The sacred marriage was a ritual between God and Goddess, which symbolized the fertility of humans, crops and animals. This ritual would be enacted annually by a priestess (embodiment of Goddess) and a selected male (which later in history became the King). In the beginning the male was sacrificed after the ritual and later it was purely symbolic.

One example of a Neolithic city is Catal Huyuk, Anatolia (now modern Turkey). It thrived from about 7000 to 5000 B.C. Catal Huyuk is the largest Neolithic site, occupying 32 acres and was discovered in 1957 by James Mellart. It was an advanced civilization that centered on a Mother Goddess. The city was built on a plain surrounded by trees, grassland and roaming herds of animals. They had stone carving, weaving, cloth dyeing, pottery, basketwork, spinning, cultivated crops and built houses and shrines. Also there are indications of the smelting of copper and lead.

In all drawings on walls, only the Goddess is depicted, the God was represented as a bull. In many locations the Goddess is seen as giving birth to several bulls. It appears that he was both the consort and the son of the Goddess, which will be seen, in later cultures. The Goddess is depicted in her three aspects – a young girl, a woman giving birth and an old woman.

There is no indication of warfare in Catal Huyuk. There was a division of labor between the sexes but no indication of superiority. Society was basically equalitarian with no distinctions between sex and class. In temple remains, females are shown preparing and conducting Goddess rituals. Baking bread, weaving and making pottery were also relegated to women.

Around 4500 B.C. this idyllic life was interrupted by the arrival of warlike tribes of Indo-Europeans or Aryans. These tribes were nomadic and came from the North and East. They are also called Kurgans or Barrow people. They worshipped sky Gods, carried weapons such as the battleaxe and dagger and rode horses that they had domesticated. These ruthless invaders imposed their own mythology and customs on the peaceful agriculturalists. Gimbutas believes that the Kurgans invaded Europe in three waves from 4300 to 2800 B.C. These invasions all but wiped out the previous culture or assimilated it into their own. The Kurgans social system was hierarchal and dominated by powerful males and a male priesthood. They practiced human (men, women and children) sacrifice and animal sacrifice.

Another example of a high Goddess civilization that existed into the historical era is Crete. Since Crete avoided being invaded longer than other Neolithic communities it evolved without disruption until about 1450 B.C. when the second and greater of two earthquakes abruptly ended most of its civilization. In Crete the Goddess is depicted as a flowing, dynamic energy that could manifest as a swarm of bees or coils of snakes. She is usually seen with her arms raised and either serpents coiling around her arms or holding the double axes.

Crete had a prosperous trade with other countries in the Mediterranean. They exported olive oil, honey, fish, fruit and herbs. Cretan palaces were spacious and usually several stories high. They had courtyards that were decorated with images of flowers and animal life. Attention was given to beauty and details. They had a high standard of living as it seems that even the peasants had comparable living spaces.

Sir Arthur Evans excavated the palace at Knossos, Crete in the beginning of the 20th century. He discovered five great palace complexes. Evans called the culture Minoan after the Homeric legends. Their cities were organized, they had harbor installations, networks of roads, drainage systems, sanitary installations and organized temples and burial grounds. Cretan towns were not fortified and violence was never depicted in all their artwork. Finally around 1100 B.C. the succumbed to dominion under the Achaeans, but the Goddess still survived there in a lesser form.

Goddess images where found everywhere with her child or consort. The beauty of Minoan women is seen in frescos. They all wore typical Minoan dress that was bare-breasted with a long skirt, just like the Goddess statues. Women participated in all areas of society and there seemed to be no domination by either sex. Women and men can be seen working together as partners in bull-vaulting, which appears to be some sort of sport performed in honor of the Goddess. In religious ceremonies, the priestess always presided.

In Cretan art the God was depicted as a bull, he was the son-lover of the Goddess. He personified growth and had to die annually in order to be reborn. He is the form of life that changes and she is the principle that is continually renewing itself. At one time the King was sacrificed annually to be replaced by the bull. The sacrificial tool utilized was the double axe, which the Goddess is seen carrying in her most common form. Before the bull was sacrificed, its magical power was invoked by the bull vaulting event. In bull vaulting, teams would take turns grasping the horns of the bull and somersaulting over its back.

It appears that Cretan wealth was primarily spent on living harmoniously. Their art reflects a society that was not based on dominance and oppression. They seem to have diverted their aggressiveness by a well-balanced sexual life. The women were bare-breasted and the men wore skimpy clothes that emphasized their genitals. In our society today, it seems that sex can be seen as more sinful than warfare.

At the beginning of the Bronze Age around 3500 B.C., women still maintained freedoms in Goddess city-states. In Sumer and Babylonia, women married more than one man. There was no penalty for women who participated in adultery and marriage had to be approved by mother and father. Women engaged in business activities of the temple, held real estate in their own names, lent money and conducted business. The earliest accounts of writing in 3200 B.C. were discovered in the temple of Inanna for land payment. The scribes were women. Seven of Hammurabi's laws concerned the priestesses of the temple and their rights to inherit and pass on to offspring. In this time period if a woman was raped by a man, he was put to death.

In the classical age of Sparta, where Artemis was worshipped, the women were free and independent. Young Spartan women could be found in the gymnasium, where they tossed off their restrictive clothes and wrestled naked with their male counterparts. They had total sexual freedom and were encouraged to get pregnant by the most handsome man they could find (Stone, 1976).

In the Bronze Age, 3500 to 1250 B.C. is seen the beginning of the decline of the Goddess. As stated before waves of Northern invaders swept across Europe and Asia from 4300 to 2800 B.C. These invaders gradually imposed their ways of life on those they conquered. They were referred to as Indo-Europeans, Aryans in India, Hittites in the

Fertile Crescent, Luwians in Anatolia, Kurgans in Europe and Achaeans in Greece (Eisler, 1988). There were other nomadic invaders as well; the most famous were a Semitic group called Hebrews who invaded Canaan. The one thing they all had in common was a dominator model of society, in which male dominance and violence was then norm. These nomads also used metal for weapons. These metals were previously used for jewelry, ritual and tools.

What differentiates the Bronze Age from others is the advent of writing. It appears at first on clay and strips of papyrus and then carved on temples and walls. Originally it was utilized to keep track of property and temple goods. Some theorists believe that the development of writing is what turned society from matriarchal to patriarchal. That will be discussed later in this paper.

Now stories and myths can be passed on through writing as opposed to oral traditions. Many of these stories were about the Goddess and her son-lover. The most common story is about the separation of the Goddess and her lover who appears to die and go the underworld. This is also reflected in the seasons. The Goddess must then descend into the darkness to retrieve her loved one and bring him into the light. This can also be seen as a metaphor for change.

In Sumeria, the Goddess Inanna must go to the underworld and meet her sister Ereshkigal, who makes her submit to trials. When Inanna returns she sends her consort Dumuzi to take her place. In Babylonia the Goddess is called Ishtar and her son-lover is Tammuz. In Egypt she is Isis and her brother-lover is Osiris. In Canaan, it is the God Baal who must be retrieved by his sister Anath. In Greece it is the story of Persephone being kidnapped by Hades and finally returned her to her mother Demeter.

Towards the middle of the Bronze Age the Goddess seems to recede into the background as the father Gods take center stage. The new creation myths in which the God plays the major role now overshadow the old ones. In the new myths, heaven and earth are separated and the God orders from beyond instead of a Goddess who moves from within. The hero myth now becomes popular. It shifts the focus away from the Goddess.

Now the surviving Goddesses take on a new image, Goddess of war. Goddesses are now depicted as carrying weapons and leading armies into battle to conquer enemies. Goddesses are also depicted as bestowing power to the ruling king or the king is said to have been the son of the Goddess or incarnation of the God/son-lover.

Isis was one of the three great Goddesses of the Bronze Age; the others were Cybele of Anatolia and Inanna of Sumeria. Isis was the greatest and most popular of all Goddesses worshipped in Egypt. She was worshipped for over 3000 years (Baring, 1993). Her images passed to Mary around the 2ND century B.C. Her sphere of influence covered not only Egypt but Greece and Roman Empire.

She was known as the milk-giving cow Goddess, Goddess of serpents, star Goddess Sirius who brought about the annual flooding of the Nile, the fertile pig Goddess, bird Goddess, Goddess of the Underworld who gave the breath of life to the dead, Tree of Life, mother of Horus, Goddess of the throne upon whose lap the king sat. She was the Great Mother Goddess from whom all Gods and Goddesses were born but she was also born from the Earth and the Sky.

Isis is seen as a sympathetic Goddess due to her search for her husband/brother Osiris. The myth of Isis and Osiris begins with Osiris being first king of Egypt and Isis his wife. Osiris is credited with being creator of civilization, agriculture and establishing justice. Isis ruled in his absence.

Their brother Seth became jealous of Osiris and tricked him into getting inside a chest, which was then sealed and thrown, into the Nile. Isis mourns and searches for the chest containing Osiris and finds it in Phoenicia. It was lodged in a tree, which grew around it. The tree is cut down by a local king to be made into a pillar in his palace. She recovers the chest and incarnates her husband with her wings and becomes pregnant with his son Horus. Seth later finds chest and tears Osiris into pieces. Isis with help of her sister Nephthys (Seth's wife) again finds Osiris' body and with all formality in funeral rites reassembles him and now he becomes the Ruler of Eternity in the Underworld to judge all souls. Horus later takes his father's place as ruler of Earth with his mother Isis.

Symbolically, Isis became pregnant with the rebirth of Osiris, Horus is today and Osiris is yesterday. Osiris's gift is resurrection, but like the corn he had to die to live again. Isis and Nephthys were often depicted as having their wings spread around a pharaoh's sarcophagus beating their wings, which gave the breath of life and as protection for the dead king. Isis is usually depicted as having wings and either having the cow horns and solar disc on her head or the throne.

In a book called the *Golden Ass*, written in the 1st century B.C. an initiate of the mysteries of Isis named Apuleius describes meeting Isis (Baring, 1993). She says to him:

> I am Nature, the universal Mother, mistress of all the elements, primordial child of time, sovereign of all things spiritual, queen of the dead, queen also of the immortals, the single manifestation of all gods and goddesses that are. My nod governs the shining heights of Heaven, the wholesome sea-breezes, the lamentable silences of the world below. Though I am worshipped in many aspects, known by countless names, and propitiated with all manner of different rites, yet the whole round earth venerates me. The primeval Phrygians call me Pessinuntica, Mother of the

Gods; the Athenians, sprung from their own soil, call me Cecropian
Artemis; for the islanders of Cyprus I am Paphian Aphrodite; for the
archers of Crete I am Dyctynna; for the trilingual Sicilians, Stygian
Proserpine; and for the Eleusinians their ancient Mother of the Corn.
Some know me as Juno, some as Bellona of the Battles; others as Hecate,
others again as Rhamnubia, but both races of Aethiopians, whose lands the
morning sun first shines upon, and the Egyptians, who excel in ancient
learning and worship me with ceremonies proper to my godhead, call me
by my true name, namely Queen Isis.

Goddess worship benefited the women of Egypt in many ways. The queen always had greater power than the king and in fact it was part of the marriage contract that the husband should be obedient to his wife in all ways (Stone, 1976). The system of inheritance through mother-kin lasted until Roman times.

Women had great freedom; they went into the marketplace, transacted affairs and occupied themselves with business while their husbands stayed home to weave according to Herodotus of Greece. Love poems found in Egyptian tombs suggest that the women did the courting and oftentimes plied their men with intoxicants to weaken their protestations. At the royal level, the rules of inheritance were matrilineal, which could account for so many marriages between brothers and sisters. This allowed the son access to the family inheritance.

Parallels are seen with another Great Mother Goddess named Inanna (Ishtar). Inanna of Sumeria, modern day Iraq, was later known as Ishtar of Babylon. Inanna was depicted as wearing a horned and tiered crown with a cone inside. She has the flounced and tiered dress of all Sumerian Goddesses. She usually carries a staff intertwined with serpents (caduceus). Much of the imagery of Inanna and the myths of Sumeria were inherited by the Hebrews and Christians. Her imagery is the basis for Gnostic Sophia,

Eve, and the Jewish Shekinah. Sumerian legends speak of the Garden of Eden and the Flood.

Inanna was also known as the Queen of the Heaven and Earth, Priestess of Heaven, Light of the World, Morning and Evening Star, First Daughter of the Moon, Righteous Judge, Forgiver of Sins, Holy Shepherdess, Heirdole of Heaven and Opener of the Womb. She was considered a Virgin Queen. She shared this title later with the Virgin Mary of Christianity. Also both shared images of the crescent moon, Venus and both had a son who dies a sacrificial death, descends into the Underworld and is resurrected. Nativity scenes were also painted depicting Inanna and Dumuzi, her son-lover, with a star overhead and two figures bearing gifts.

Sumerian women were men's equals socially and economically, at least in the upper classes until the Indo-Europeans invaded and exerted their influence. A gradual decline of the Goddess is seen and she is eventually usurped by Enlil, a sky God, whose imagery is later seen in Yahweh.

Inanna is called a Virgin Goddess because life appears out of her without any union with anything external to herself. The term originally had nothing to do with sexual purity, it was more metaphysical. Inanna was also a Goddess of sexual love and fertility. As Heirodule of Heaven she was a servant of the holy. Later this was translated as prostitute, which omits the actual intention of the term.

The priestesses who served in her temple were considered the vehicles of her creative life during their sexual union with the men who came to the temple. It was a sacred rite and ritual. It was also sacred because the state of bliss achieved during sex was the closest a mortal could come to association with the divine.

Sex between the Goddess and God was called the "Sacred Marriage". It symbolized the union of the moon and sun, heaven and earth. It was usually celebrated in the spring when the God was reborn after his return from the underworld. The ritual took place in the temple bedroom at the top of the ziggurat. Usually the high priestess or queen played the role of the Goddess and the role of the God was played by the high priest or king. This ritual also renewed the fertility of the land. This will be discussed later in more detail as a psychotherapeutic technique.

With the advent of the Indo-Europeans and their male Gods, Inanna slowly became a warrior Goddess. The people of Sumeria began to build walls of defense around their cities. The legendary king Gilgamesh erected a wall around the ancient city of Uruk that was over 8 miles long, 20 feet high and 15 feet thick. Inanna is now depicted as riding the backs of two lions. From now on the power of the Goddess is invoked to help them defeat their enemies.

Cybele is the third Great Mother Goddess that actually survives into the Iron Age. Less is known about Cybele than Isis and Inanna. Cybele was a Goddess of Anatolia and later came to Rome. She is often depicted with lions. She was called the Lady of Ida and Goddess of the Mountain. She was associated with Artemis and Aphrodite. In Greek and Roman times she was called the Mother of the Gods and is associated with Demeter and Gaia. She was credited with developing agriculture and law.

Anatolia was first invaded by Hittites and later by Phyrgians but the cult of Cybele and her son-lover Attis survived. Later she was moved to Rome when a prophecy declared that her worship would save Rome from Hannibal. Cybele belonged to the Roman pantheon of Gods but seemed to stand apart as did Gaia in Greece. Cybele's public rites were orgiastic and ecstatic. They usually involved self-flagellation and self-castration while in an ecstatic trance. Usually a bull or ram was sacrificed. The Christian Holy Week coincides with the week dedicated to Cybele rites.

Little is known about Attis, the son-lover of Cybele, since the original language of Cybele's home has still not been completely interpreted. It is known that he was sacrificed annually in the spring festival for fertility reasons. The high priest was usually regarded as Attis. Attis was also associated with the popular war God Mithras.

The Greek Goddesses are the most popular of all due to poems written by Homer in the 8th century B.C. Most of the Greek Goddesses had formerly been Great Mother Goddesses in their own rights or were one and the same but with the invasions of warrior tribes they were separated and their powers were assumed by male Gods.

Zeus was a Father God of the sky. In Greek mythology he was married to Hera and she was reduced to an ineffective, jealous wife. Her stories are older than his indicating that she was a former Mother Goddess. By marrying her, Zeus annexed some of her powers. The Goddesses were still worshipped in their own rights but now the world was patriarchal.

Artemis is perhaps one of the oldest Greek Goddesses. As Goddess of the hunt, she harkens back to the Paleolithic times before agriculture. She was a Virgin Goddess and personified the new moon. She had a great temple at Ephesus. Over 1000 years later, Mary, mother of Jesus would be declared Mother of God in Ephesus.

Athena was the Virgin Warrior Goddess. She was depicted with a shield, helmet and girdle. She was the Guardian of Athens. Earlier pictures of her show a wild Goddess wreathed in snakes. She was born by bursting forth from Zeus's forehead. This established a Father-right as opposed to the older Mother-right.

Aphrodite is also considered an original Mother Goddess. She was born from the separation of the Earth and Heaven, the beginning of the process of creation. She came to Greece from Cyprus and before that from Mesopotamia so her legend is very old. She is new in Olympia and plays a diminished role.

As Goddess of love and beauty she is irresistible to humans, Gods and animals. The only ones who are not affected by her power are Athena, Artemis and Hestia. She is associated with the morning star, Venus, much as Inanna was. She will become Astarte in Phoenicia and Ashtoreth by the Hebrews.

As Goddess of love she was also involved in the ritual of temple "prostitution", a service offered freely on her behalf. Aphrodite also has a lover who is called Adonis. He is killed in a hunting accident.

Demeter is another Mother Goddess. She is the Corn Mother, the Goddess of the harvest and fertility. Her daughter Persephone is the Corn Maiden. Persephone is the reborn Demeter. The most famous myth is about the kidnapping of Persephone by Hades. While Persephone was held in the underworld, her mother Demeter mourned and nothing grew on earth. Finally when Persephone was returned so did fertility to the earth, but since Persephone had eaten some pomegranate seeds in the underworld she was fated to return annually for half the year, hence the seasons.

Demeter's festivals were celebrated at the changing of the seasons, in the fall and in the spring. It is believed that Demeter was worshipped in Crete prior to being imported to Greece. Demeter is responsible for the mysteries of Eleusis, mysteries that relate to agriculture. These rites were attended by women only. At the time of the fall festival, the Thesmophoria, the women had to be sexually abstinent and a pig sacrifice was involved. It also included the use of menstrual blood in fertilizing the fields (Kraemer, 2004).

In the Iron Age (1250 B.C.) the patriarchal religions rise and all but extinguish the Goddess. In Hebrew mythology, God, known as Yahweh-Elohim created the heaven and the earth alone. He had no family and no wife or child. This world does not spring forth from his body like the Goddess but from his word. He has no image and is represented by a disembodied voice. The Father God is not only elevated above the Mother Goddess; He becomes supreme as if a Mother Goddess never existed.

There are many similarities between Hebrew mythology and Babylonian mythology. This could be because the Hebrews were exiled in Babylonia for some time. Babylonian myth tells of an evil Goddess name Tiamat (former Mother Goddess) who was defeated by male God Marduk. The Hebrews would have been familiar with Babylonian myth as they would have had the opportunity to hear the stories in the temple of Marduk every spring.

Yahweh constantly struggles against cosmic forces that threaten his rule, forces which are usually depicted as female and relate the Goddess Tiamat or Ishtar or a serpent, which formerly represented the Goddess. In the Old Testament version of the creation and the flood, there was no Mother Goddess mentioned as in previous Sumerian and Babylonian versions. This could be due to the Hebrews contempt of Ishtar who they called the Great Whore of Babylon.

Yahweh is described as a transcendent God. He is above and beyond his people, not a part of them as the Goddess was, immanent. He protects them but they must obey his laws. Also image-making is forbidden. Goddesses relied on image as opposed to word, which will be discussed at length later in this paper. The divine is no longer seen in nature and it is beyond all created things. Since Yahweh had no form, he also had no name. For one who is transcendent, Yahweh appears to be very human. He is jealous, vengeful and expresses both anger and kindness.

Yahweh is uniquely male. There is no female to temper his maleness. A true universal deity cannot take sides, but Yahweh is seen as ordering the slaughter of other peoples. This is more similar to tribal warrior Gods seen in the mode of the Aryan invaders. His power is unchecked by a female Goddess. This also reflects the priesthood of the time as there were no Hebrew priestesses. Yahweh's demands and commandments are more easily understood when seen in the context of Iron Age values and patriarchal customs.

The women of Canaan were subjected to Hebrew law and lost many of their rights. No woman could have money or property upon divorce since her word was invalid. Since she could not make an oral vow, she could not engage in business. By Hebrew law, a woman was to be stoned or burned to death for losing her virginity before marriage and if she was raped, a single woman was forced to marry the rapist. If she was already betrothed or married she was to be stoned to death for having been raped (Stone, 1976).

Finally in the 3rd century B.C., the image of the Sophia, the feminine aspect of deity, also known as wisdom comes into being perhaps to temper the ethical discipline of the father with the compassion of the mother. Prior to this the only feminine influence is seen in the female cherubim, who are depicted with wings spread around Ark of the

Covenant, strangely reminiscent of Egyptian Isis and Nephthys. This emergence of Sophia speaks of a need to resolve the image of the complementary feminine principle.

There were Canaanite Goddesses but few of their images have survived destruction by the Hebrews. The most well known is Asherah. She was probably the oldest and is compared to Isis. She was originally seen as the wife of Yahweh by the Hebrew people when he assimilated the imagery of her husband El. Her children were Baal and Anath. Kings were nourished at her breast. She was usually depicted with the Tree of Life. There are many references to a constant struggle in the Old Testament to draw the people away from worship of Asherah, but her worship continued sporadically. Some small clay figures of her have been found in excavations indicating that women may have appealed to her during childbirth or for fertility.

Many of the Hebrew prophets and priests saw it as their duty to turn their people away from the Goddess worship, both for political reasons and due to Yahweh's decree against idols. The "holy war" against the Goddess now becomes a holy war between masculine and feminine.

Not only were the images of the Goddess forbidden, but law prohibited the men from participating in the custom of intercourse with the temple priestesses and for the care of the children that resulted from these unions. Patrilineal descent guaranteed under threat of death by requiring daughters to be virgin (physically) before marriage and that wives "belonged" to their husbands.

Whenever people wandered and worshipped the Goddess, catastrophes were blamed on this indiscretion. The women of the time did offer some resistance and blamed their problems on the fact that they had been ordered to cease worshipping the Queen of Heaven and not Yahweh.

As stated in the beginning in a quote that Genesis was the beginning of the end for the Goddess, Eve's actions brought about a change of state, separation from the divine, which puts humans into the cycle of birth and death. The myth was originally a local and historical myth, which has been taken out of context and is seen now as an eternal statement. This statement is later interpreted literally and the "sin of Eve" is generalized to all women. This has had far-reaching implications for the rejected feminine principle.

The story of Eve is also the story of the displacement of the Mother Goddess. Death, which was once only a phase in life, is now seen as a final punishment. It is an act contrary to nature, which the Goddess represents; just as Eve is born from Adam's rib instead of natural birth from a womb. The symbolism in the myth is also representative of the Goddess – the serpent and the Tree of Life.

Eve is seen as bringing death, sin and pain to humankind. She is blamed for all humankind being born in sin forever after. Women are depicted as inherently evil and sinful and luring men into sin. Eve is the body, matter and carnality whereas Adam is mind, spirit and spirituality. Eve is also seen as inferior since she was created second. She touched the divine only through Adam. Eve was more likely to be tempted since she was weaker. She was seen as morally weak, less rational, less disciplined, vain, greedy and cunning. She is more instinctive and sexual. Sex was considered a gateway for the devil to enter.

Later Aristotle and Thomas Aquinas would write that woman was merely the passive vessel that held the child of the man and brought it to birth and that the man contributed semen and therefore the child was his. At the time they did not fully understand the human reproductive system and its cooperative effort between male and female.

Sex was seen as sinful and chastity was honored as the way to mortality by the Christian fathers. The body was denigrated and since it represented woman, she also was denigrated. Man and woman were condemned to sin eternally. There was no inherent good in the natural world or human nature.

Jesus of Nazareth associated freely with women, he even had one in his rank of disciples, Mary Magdalene. He denounced the patriarchal ruling class and said that the meek shall inherit the earth. He preached universal love. Perhaps Jesus was a feminist. He elevated feminine values.

Since Jesus was seen as the second Adam, Mary was seen as the second Eve. It is through Mary's virginity that the sin of Eve was redeemed. It was necessary for Jesus to be born by immaculate conception to be free of the original sin of the mother's womb. Virginity was identified as sinless which implied that sexuality was the primary sin. The ultimate effect on women was to try to identify themselves with Mary, if they could not then they must identify with Eve who was sinful. There was no way for an ordinary woman to resolve the opposing roles of virgin and mother.

Not much about Mary's birth or death is mentioned in the New Testament, but she can be called the unrecognized Mother Goddess of the Christian tradition. Within 500 years of her death she assumes a pantheon images from previous Goddesses – Aphrodite, Cybele, Demeter, Isis, Hathor, Inanna and Astarte. She is both a virgin and a mother, she has a son who is half divine, and he dies and is resurrected after a journey to the Underworld.

In 431 A.D. at the Council of Ephesus, Mary was proclaimed as the God-bearer by the Christian fathers. This is the same town where the great temple of Artemis had stood for centuries. The cult of Artemis had been repressed in 380 A.D. and it seems that the people deprived of their Goddess, readily and instinctually turned to Mary instead. Everywhere former Goddess temples were dedicated to churches for the Virgin Mary. Feasts of the Virgin were celebrated in different countries.

Mary's cult reached its height in the Middle Ages in France, when over 180 churches and cathedrals were built in her honor. The Protestants, however, did not acknowledge her divine nature. Mary was later called the Queen of Heaven but since she was never the Queen of the Earth and born human, she is technically not a Mother Goddess, but was the closest that was allowed to be worshipped. Still, there were over 21,000 visions of Mary recorded in the last 1000 years (Baring, 1993). Many churches were constructed on the site of a vision such as Lourdes.

Another similarity of Mary to the Goddesses before her was that birth of Jesus was celebrated on the 25th of December. For thousands of years this was the time of the Winter Solstice, celebrated as the birth of the sun God. The Solstice is the longest night of the year, which usually occurs on the 21st. The light of the God pierces the darkness and insures that the seasons will continue to turn. Just as the star announced the birth of Jesus, the star Sirius announced the flooding of the Nile and the birth of Osiris.

Another Mary of the New Testament that is worth mentioning is Mary Magdalene. There is much mystery that surrounds her. Was she a penitent whore or was she one of the disciples or was she the wife of Jesus? She anointed Jesus at the last supper in the tradition of the Goddess and she was present during his resurrection ritual as past Goddesses presided over rebirth.

The Gnostic Gospels proclaim that Jesus and Mary were in love and were married. There is even a theory that she was pregnant with Jesus' child and fled to France where the Cathars later protected and honored her line. This appears to be symbolic of the Sacred Marriage of the God and Goddess. Mary also symbolized the Holy Grail.

Gnostic Christianity through its image of Sophia as the embodiment of wisdom saw Sophia as the Great Mother, a consort of the male aspect of the Godhead. Gnostic traditions were suppressed in 326 A.D. but saw a brief resurgence in the Middle Ages with the devotion of Mary, the Cathars, the Holy Grail search and the Black Madonnas. This reveals the constant attempt on some level to reconcile masculine and feminine.

The Gospels that were included in the New Testament do not mention anything about the feminine Sophia. The psychic ground, feminine aspect, was split off from the intellect, masculine aspect. The Church chose to depict itself as the bride of Christ, but just as the masculine, the feminine also demands a personal representation. Gnostic Christianity has its roots in Egyptian, Greek and Hebrew religions. There was a climate of tolerance and their views towards other religions were very liberal.

The group of Gnostics (knowledge gained through intuition) was established by James, known as Jesus' brother. They were concerned with the nature of the universe, the origin of evil, and the fall and redemption of the soul. They felt the essence of Jesus' teaching was to transmit the knowledge of the heart. They attempted to awaken the soul to its divine awareness.

In the creation myth of the Gnostics, the mother Sophia gave birth to a daughter, also Sophia, who lost contact with her heavenly origin and in her distress, brought the earth into being. She became lost and entangled in this chaotic realm. She could not return to the realm of light so the Mother sends her son Christ to rescue her. Christ descends into the darkness to awaken his sister to remember her true nature. As a metaphor this story describes the soul and its compelling drive to reincarnate until it remembers its home and desires to return. So humanity is not evil but unconscious.

Gnostics described their God as both father and mother. The image of the Sacred Marriage is seen throughout the Gnostic texts recovered at Nag Hammadi, it is their most important sacrament. The reunion and return to the divine realm is celebrated in the Sacred Marriage. It manifests as the two halves of the soul, the masculine and the feminine. The Holy Spirit is referred to as feminine in Gnostic texts.

In the Gnostic Church, women could teach, heal, prophesy and hold any rank that men did, including bishop. This greatly irritated the orthodox Christians, who called them heretics. The only other church that allowed this was the Cathar Church of the Holy Spirit, which allowed women to hold rank, administer the sacraments, teach, baptize and heal the sick. This seems strange when up until the Bronze Age women had been priestesses in the temples of the Goddess. How deeply has this wounded women's souls and curtailed her growth as human beings? With no image of women in any sacred role in society how could women relate on a personal level to the archetypal feminine?

The Gnostic tradition was forced to go underground but resurfaced in the 12th century in France and Northern Spain and their connection with the Cathar Church of the Holy Spirit and the Knights Templar. The Gnostic ideas were spread by troubadours singing about the quest for the Holy Grail. The troubadours sang about courtly love and offered a new image for men that of being gentle, courtly and cultivated. They began to free sexuality and eroticism from guilt.

The feminine idea once again becomes a focus of consciousness. The emphasis was not on the Goddess but on Sophia. In the courts of France women were celebrated for their beauty, compassion and intelligence. They had a social role outside of being a wife and only experiencing sex during procreation. Unfortunately their vision was all but wiped out during the Albigensian Crusade against the Cathar "heresy." The Templars had similar beliefs and even allowed women into their ranks. They were destroyed with barbaric cruelty in 1309 by the church.

The Holy Grail, the cup that Jesus drank from at the last supper and the cup that caught his blood during the crucifixion was also a metaphor for the Divine Feminine. The grail symbolizes the womb. Those that went on the quest in search of the Grail were transformed in the Gnostic notion. It is the soul's reunion with its Divine Ground.

While history marched on in Europe and the Mediterranean, the Goddess fared differently in India. Hindu scriptures make no mention of original sin, a fall or redemption, no Eve is responsible for the loss of paradise and no God decrees that man shall rule over woman (Pattanaik, 2000). Instead, Goddesses abound in Hindu temples.

In the Hindu Vedas, sacred texts, written between 1500 B.C and 1000 B.C., the Goddesses are minor characters. Most of the Gods at the time were warrior Gods, possibly due to the Aryan invasions. The pre-Vedic Goddesses that survived were mainly fertility Goddesses. In later Hinduism the idea of a Mahadevi or Great Goddess flourished. The earliest mention of a supreme Goddess was in the 5th century A.D. in a text called *Devi-Mahatmya*, or the Glorification of the Goddess. It contains hymns of praise.

The earliest statue or carving of a fertility supreme Goddess is from the 7th century A. D. She is divine because of her ability to bring forth life. She is usually depicted squatting and nude with a lotus covering her head. The male role, though vital, is momentary. The female womb does all of the work. The male analyzes and the female nourishes. Women must accept their biology but men do not have to.

In the Hindu worldview, birth and death are alternating events. Death is not the end but a transition until another body can be obtained so the spirit or soul can continue to experience and grow. The quality of the body depends on deeds done in the past life; this is referred to as karma. Karma rotates the cycle of life. Release from karma comes only with the realization that the true self is not the ego but the spirit within. Life is an opportunity to fulfill karmic obligations or debt.

Man is the keeper of spirit and woman is the mistress of matter. A paradigm was created that prejudiced attitudes towards femininity forever. Women were associated with passive matter that is animated by male spirit.

Matter and soul, like man and woman complement each other. Women were the left halves and men were the right halves. Fertility cults that give women dominance like Tantra were called left-handed paths.

The Hindu godhead was comprised of Brahma, who creates, Vishnu, who sustains and Shiva, who destroys. They did not rule alone, they had consorts who provided them their power. Brahma's consort was Sarasvati, Goddess of knowledge. Vishnu's consort was Laxmi or Laksmi, Goddess of wealth. Shiva's consort was Shakti or Kali, Goddess of death or destruction.

Sarasvati was originally a river Goddess but today is worshipped as a Goddess of knowledge. Her fertility became more cerebral as she is now giver of imagination and creativity. She is associated with speech and all knowledge both sacred and secular originates with her (Trobe, 2000).

Kali, the consort of Shiva, is described as a Goddess of death. She is naked except for a necklace of human heads and a skirt of human arms. She has 4-10 arms; her skin is black and is covered in blood. She gives and she destroys, she is inevitable like death or disease. Kali is intoxicated by bloodlust, when she is activated she is terrible and difficult to stop.

Laksmi is depicted in the Vedas as the Goddess of status, wealth and sovereignty. She blesses brides and consecrates marriages. She is usually depicted with golden coins, elephants and sitting on a lotus blossom.

In the Hindu worldview, the woman gave the man access to pleasure, in pleasure he acquires a family and is lord of the household, which gives him the moral right to own property. Without a woman, a man can only be a student or celibate hermit. Only as a householder do the Gods bestow gifts on the man. Man owes a debt to his ancestors so he must produce children so that they can be reborn.

Fathers were concerned about the welfare of their daughters and would not give them in marriage to men who were weak or had loose morals. The wealth that came with the wife was hers alone. In ancient India the women were allowed to choose their own husband. The wife reflected on the husband. If the wife was beautiful, happy and richly adorned then his prestige was high. The number of happy women in his harem determined his worldly power. Rape was not condoned but attempting to abort a fetus was considered a greater sin. Killing a woman was also a great sin because it in essence kills all the children she will ever bear.

Many of the Goddesses in India have two sides, a good compassionate side and a destructive side. This paradox reflects their region where life depends on the equilibrium of two antagonistic forces, fire and water, drought and flood.

In the Far East it is difficult to discern the Goddess, perhaps because this is where the nomadic invaders may have originated. It does appear that there was a sun Goddess cult in China, Korea and Japan dedicated to the Goddess Ameratsu. She rules the heavens and brings warmth and light to the world (Hunt, 2001). She is responsible for cultivating rice fields, creating irrigation canals and teaching the arts of weaving, cultivating silk and food. She does not seem to have much influence on mortal women as the Asian societies are very patriarchal.

Next various reasons for this shift to patriarchy will be examined.

DECLINE OF THE GODDESS

One can only wonder what civilization would have been like if the Goddess cultures of the Bronze Age had continued to evolve uninterrupted. There are several theories as to why this shift occurred. First and foremost is the arrival of the Northern invaders. Sometimes this theory is coupled with natural disasters that weakened the indigenous peoples further. Another interesting theory is the advent of the written language. And lastly that patriarchy was necessary for the development of humankind.

The most popular theory is the invasion of the peaceful Goddess cultures by warrior cults. These migratory warrior tribesmen imposed their mythology and their patriarchal customs on the agricultural peoples whose territory they invaded. They brought with them sky Gods along with weapons like the mace and the battle axe and rode horses and chariots. They are the Indo-European (Aryan) and Semitic cultures. Their impact was felt from Europe to India.

The mythology of the Goddess was radically transformed or suppressed by the patriarchal warriors. There were two insurgent warrior waves, the Indo-Europeans in ever-increasing numbers force their way into Mesopotamia, Anatolia and other lands eastwards towards India and the Semitic tribes move into Mesopotamia and the Canaan from the Syro-Arabian desert.

The Paleolithic hunters of the grassy steppes north of the Caspian and Black Seas have now become warriors and seek the more prosperous lands to the South. Wherever they penetrated they established themselves as the ruling caste. Their appearance is marked by a trail of destruction. In Anatolia alone over 300 cities were sacked and burned; among them was Troy in 2300 B.C. (Baring, 1993). They considered themselves superior to the more cultured, peaceful farmers.

They were known as Hittites in Anatolia and Syria; Mittani, Hurrians and Kassites in Mesopotamia; Achaeans and Dorians in Greece and Aryans in the Indus Valley.

The Aryans were predominantly a society of warriors; they were polygamous, patriarchal, tent dwellers that were filthy and tough. They herded cattle, rode horses and invented the spoked wheel and chariot about 2000-1750 B.C. They buried their tribal leaders beneath a mound with sacrificed attendants and horses as the Kurgans had done before them. Their sky Gods were Gods of lightning, storm, wind, sun and fire. Their tribal myths were transmitted orally by priests. Writing was forbidden.

To the west of Mesopotamia in the great desert from Syria to southern Arabia emerged the Semitic tribes. Among these tribes were the Akkadians, the Amoritic Babylonians whose famous leader was Hammurabi. They were succeeded by the Canaanites and the Hebrews. Later the Assyrians took over the Hebrews in Babylon.

Both groups of invaders introduced the idea of an opposition of light and dark. This imposed a polarity upon the Goddess cultures, which had encompassed all as one. Nature and human life is desacralized. The Goddess cultures lived close to the soil and experienced the Goddess as immanent in all life.

As a result of the Aryan and Semitic invasions, attitudes towards life and death were also changed. Life was untrustworthy and violent death became the norm. People no longer felt safe in their villages and large fortified cities were built. This warrior ethos compelled kings to take over more territory. This pattern of war and conflict has endured until today.

The moral order of the Goddess culture was based on a relationship of all beings; the moral order of the God culture was based on opposition and conquest. These political changes were seen in the changing positions of the Goddesses. Where once they ruled alone, now they had son-lovers, later they were married to Gods who usurped their powers and eventually the Gods ruled alone. The women of the time lost all of their freedoms too. Women were regarded as property and sons inherited from their fathers with nothing for the daughters.

Sometimes the female deity was symbolized as a serpent or dragon or some kind of evil being that the God, King or hero must defeat. One prime example of the defeat of the Goddess is the Babylonian myth of Tiamat and Marduk.

The Babylonian epic of creation tells the story of the conquest and murder of the original mother Goddess Tiamat by her great grandson Marduk. The epic tells of how the Gods were brought into being by the primal mother Tiamat and the primal father Apsu. Conflict arises between the new and older generation and eventually the newer generation overthrows the older ones.

Tiamat turns from a mother Goddess into a death-dealing dragon and gives birth to a brood of monster serpents. Marduk opposed Tiamat and her monster serpents. He was given an invincible weapon, the thunderbolt. He also summoned the winds to help him in battle. Driving a chariot, he approached Tiamat in battle.

No detail is spared in how he defeated and killed Tiamat. Marduk uses her mutilated body to create heaven and earth and her blood to create man to serve the Gods. He took from her the tablets of law.

The God in this myth embodied the powers of creation and the Goddess the powers of destruction. The Goddess who created from her body is now replaced with a God who creates outside of his body. In earlier times it was the Goddess who was the eternal source that gave birth to the son who was created in time and must die back into the source. Now the God destroys the source to become the source himself. The defeat of the Goddess marked the end of a culture and the end of the Neolithic way of perceiving life.

The new mythic model expressed by a God is one of mastery and control. It is one of desiring to shape and order what has been created. There seems to be a need in this new myth to have influence over the environment and to extend territory by war and conflict. It is now a warrior's experience of life – heroic, combative and aggressive. Emphasis is on victory in battle.

This new imagery states that what is feminine is chaotic, destructive, and demonic and is to be feared and mastered. The importance of this imagery influences Zoroastrianism, Judaism, Christianity and Islam. It has also influenced literature, science and psychology. This will be discussed in more detail later in this paper.

The second important and very innovative theory on the reason for the change to patriarchy is presented by Leonard Shlain (1998) in his book titled *The Alphabet Versus the Goddess.* Shlain proposes that the plunge in women's status and the advent of harsh patriarchy and misogyny occurred around the time that people were learning how to read and write. He believes that this new skill restructured the brain. When a critical mass of people within a society acquire literacy, left hemispheric modes of thought are reinforced at the expense of right hemispheric modes. This manifests as a decline in the status of images, women's rights and Goddess worship.

Shlain equates the right side of the brain as having feminine qualities and the left side of the brain as having masculine qualities. Shlain proposes that a holistic, simultaneous, synthetic and concrete view of the world are essential to a feminine outlook. A linear, sequential, reductionist and abstract way of thinking describes the masculine outlook. Each individual possesses both modes of perception like the ancient yin/yang symbol.

Images approximate reality, they are *concrete*. The brain simultaneously perceives all parts of the *whole* integrating the parts s*ynthetically* into a gestalt. The majority of images are perceived all at once. When reading, the words are arranged in a *linear sequence,* so the brain must *reduce* it to its components. Since the alphabetic symbols have no meaning they are *abstract*. So images are feminine and words are masculine.

In Neolithic agrarian times, a Mother Goddess was the principal deity. She was the creatrix of life, nurturer of young and protector of children and the source of milk herds, grains and vegetables. She presided over birth and death. Her consort was a smaller, younger, weaker male. Then the Goddess began to lose power. Her consort rapidly gained size and power until he usurped her sovereignty. This all started when a Sumerian invented writing by pressing a sharp stick into wet clay.

The Old Testament, its words and its three religions Judaism, Christianity and Islam are all examples of patriarchy. Each religion has an imageless Father God whose word leads to law codes, dualism and objective science. Whenever a culture values written word above image, masculinity reigns. Whenever image is valued above word, femininity reigns.

The right brain is the oldest and develops first in utero. It is nonverbal, integrates feelings, recognizes images, appreciates music, is intuitive, sustains altered states of consciousness and utilizes metaphor. The right brain is better at perceiving space and making judgments as to balance, harmony and gestalts, which are utilized in distinguishing between ugly and beautiful.

The left brain's functions are opposite and complementary to the right. The left side of the brain is concerned with doing and willing and its body side, the right side, along with the right hand throws spears and forages for food. The left knows the world through speech, 90% of language skills are in the left lobe. The left side analyzes in a linear progression. It is capable of abstract thought like freedom and justice. It is capable of logic like if-then circumstances as opposed to intuition. It is also capable of higher math like algebra.

Shlain believes that evolution caused men to be separated from their right brains; that it was necessary for men who were engaged in the dangerous activity of hunting to shut out their emotions so they wouldn't be distracted. This dispassion allowed the hunters to kill their prey. Whereas women needed access to the right brain in order to nurture and raise children.

When agriculture was developed it required some psychological reprogramming for men. It was not very exciting for men who were used to hunting wild animals to survive. It was not only women who prayed to the Goddess but men who believed her fertility extended to the crops and animals as well.

Around 4500 B.C. the first Northern warrior tribes are thought to have swept out of the Russian steppes to invade the peaceful Goddess cultures. Warriors and their sky Gods took over the Goddess cultures. These warriors had a preponderance of left brain values and they dominated the right brain Goddess cultures. The Goddess was replaced with the God.

47

Shlain does not believe that the Kurgans were solely responsible for the overthrow of the Goddess since there is very little information on the Kurgans. He feels that whenever a primitive people (Kurgans) come into contact with a more advanced people (Goddess cultures); the result is that the primitives are absorbed into the advanced society. For example, when Rome conquered Greece it adopted Greece's more sophisticated ways and its Gods. When the Mongols advanced on Baghdad in the 14th century, the city was completely destroyed but Islam continued as a religion.

Other theories proclaim the downfall of the Goddess is due to bride barter among tribes or the concept of private property. Once women began to be viewed as property, men began to control them. Shlain again believes these theories don't adequately explain the 5000 year dominance of patriarchy.

He believes that the changes occurred from inside and not outside. He believes that the central factor in the fall of the Goddess was due to literacy. First writing and then the alphabet shifted the culture's view of reality.

In Paleolithic times, man had pictographs and then petroglyphs and then around 3000 B.C. a distinctive form of writing was developed in Mesopotamia and Egypt. The Sumerians who lived between the Tigris and the Euphrates Rivers needed a way to keep track of their commerce. They made wedge-shaped forms in wet clay and cuneiform was invented. Cuneiform became gradually more abstract. When the Akkadians conquered the Sumerians the writing changed and became more phonetic and abstract. Words were arranged linearly and by 2300 B.C. were written from left to right. The language remained difficult because of the large number of characters.

The Sumerians believed that writing was a gift from the Goddess Nisaba, a Goddess of Grain. The Akkadians attributed writing to the God Nabu, God of writing. At this time Sumerian women were held in high regard. But around 1700 B.C. the creation myths of Babylon were read every spring and depicted the story of the defeat of the Goddess Tiamat by the God Marduk.

Marduk worship began around 1700 B.C., which is the same approximate date of the Babylonian King Hammurabi and his written law code in cuneiform. Patriarchy is the dominant theme of Hammurabi's Code. The ascendancy of the written laws seems to coincide with the decline of the Goddess. Grammar and laws are the purview of the left brain.

Now Egyptians developed a pictorial script called hieroglyphs. Hieroglyphs first appeared around 3000 B.C. Each glyph represented the image of a thing or action and stood for a syllable. Hieroglyphs required some skill as an artist.

Egypt's creation stories were benign compared to Babylon. They involved female deities who emerged out of chaos. Fifteen hundred years later we see one male deity, Atum as creating the popular Egyptian deities we recognize today, Isis, Osiris, Horus, Seth and Nephthys.

For a short time, the Egyptians were invaded and ruled by the Hyksos, which influenced their writing style and later under the rule of Akhenaton a third type of writing was introduced. Akhenaton did away with the pantheon and tried to force the people to worship one God, Amon. Akhenaton was the first monotheist. This new religion did not last long since the new God had no image and hieroglyphs were mostly based on images.

The societies of Egypt and Mesopotamia allow Shlain's theory to be tested. These two society's attitudes towards women were as widely divergent as was their writing. The Egyptians had joyous festivals and erotic art. Their religion was based on magic and pageantry as opposed to obligations and morality. Premarital customs were free and easy compared to the Mesopotamians. Even though their chief God was Amon, the common people preferred Isis, the Great Mother. Isis was not a Goddess of war.

Women in Mesopotamia progressively lost power, while in Egypt the women retained their high position. The women in Egypt roamed the streets unattended, ate, drank and conducted business in the open. Wives exerted some authority over their husbands and property usually passed through the mother. Egyptian love poems suggest that the women proposed marriage.

The Mesopotamians excelled in war, laws, cruelty, morality and conquest. They passed laws that sons must honor their fathers. The Babylonians had no art, sculpture or notable architecture. They made swords whereas the Egyptians made jewelry out of their metal. Women descended into servitude in Mesopotamia and Egyptian women maintained the highest status in the Western world. Shlain believes that the only clear distinction between the two cultures that would account for this difference is their form of writing. The Mesopotamians invented an abstract and linear form of writing and the Egyptians developed a concrete form of writing that used images.

The split between word and image became more evident with the invention of the alphabet. Shlain credits the Canaanites with its earlier development in 1600 B.C. as opposed to the popularly credited Phoenicians.

The most widely read and influential written record is the Bible. The oldest sections of the Bible where written between 1000 and 900 B.C. with later sections being added over the next millennium. In 367 A.D. the Christians canonized the New Testament and acknowledged the Old Testament as part of their own story. Subsequently so did the Muslims. So the Old Testament values of monotheism, rule by law and ethical living became universal values.

Since there were no images of God, people worshipped his word. The inner sanctum contained no likeness of the God only written words. This was the first time in history that a religion demanded that its people be literate. Yahweh despised the worship of images so the Israelites considered themselves to be superior to those who continued to worship idols.

Many groups profited from this new culture. They included common folk, poor, priests, warriors, judges, businessmen, sons, fathers and husbands. Those who lost ground and/or suffered were wives, queens, daughters, rape victims, female slaves, sexually adventuresome people and priestesses.

When the alphabet was brought to Greek we see stories of heroes defeating serpents (symbolism of the Goddess). One such story is the myth of Apollo defeating the serpent and establishing his temple in the place of a former Goddess temple. Apollo takes the gift of prophecy from this Mother Goddess and establishes the temple at Delphi.

The state of women can be further demonstrated in the Greek play *The Eumenides,* in which Orestes is on trial for avenging the death of his father by murdering his mother. Apollo argues that Orestes is not guilty because his duty to his father supersedes his duty to his mother. He further argues that the mother plays a very minor role. The father is the active principle and the mother is the passive vessel, so a mother is not related to her son by blood.

Another fact contributing to the downfall of the Goddess occurred around the 5th and 6th centuries B. C. with several different schools of thought that were contemporaneous. Isaiah, Socrates, Zoroaster, Buddha, Lao-tzu and Confucius were all philosophers or religious men that can claim vast influence even today.

All six had some striking similarities – each of them developed or refined an abstract system of thought that challenged the left brains, all were literate and none of them had a relationship with a woman that he valued above solitude or the company of men. It appears that men of the time obsessed with the written word tended to be sexist. Their new ideas occurred at a time when the Goddess was rapidly losing power.

Women had a glimmer of hope when Jesus of Nazareth began preaching feminine values, unfortunately it was short-lived. Jesus was cryptic and his teachings were mysterious. His parables encouraged right-brained thinking. He taught equality, nonviolence, mercy and compassion. Money, possessions and the law were irrelevant. None of his teachings were written down in his lifetime. He instructed his disciples to memorize his teachings.

After the Fall of Rome came the Dark Ages, when only the Church maintained literacy. During this time we see the rise of the cult of Mary. Many pagan temples were rededicated to the Virgin Mary. It was her image that was worshipped. This came to a crescendo in the Middle Ages. As discussed previously it was extinguished by the Church through the Crusades, the Inquisition and the Protestant Reformation.

The High Middle Ages was a time for literacy again. With the advent of the printing press, books became more accessible, especially the Bible. This also had an effect on women of the time. The Inquisition and its manual the *Malleous Maleficorum* (Witches Hammer) of 1487 brought about the death of heretics, proclaimed witches and the insane. Approximately 80% of those killed and tortured were women.

With the Protestant Reformation by Luther and Calvin in the 16th century, it was proclaimed that all should have access to the Bible. Luther relied heavily on the wrathful passages of the Old Testament. He also rejected the devotion to Mary. He believed that women should be obedient to their men and he especially disliked learned women.

Calvin followed in the same lines but was stricter. He banned all images including the crucifix. He forbade worship of Mary. He believed that women were tainted because of Eve's Original Sin so all of Eve's descendants were to submit without complaint to their husbands and fathers. Eventually all dancing, singing, bells, incense, playing cards, entertainment, drunkenness and boisterous behavior were also banned.

Women were harshly regimented and not allowed to wear lace, rouge, jewelry or colorful clothes. Sex before marriage was punishable by exile or drowning. Adultery, blasphemy, idolatry, heresy and witchcraft were punishable by death and torture was used to extract confessions. Women were not allowed in the organization of the new church. What were missing from the new Church were feminine values such as joy, love, mercy and beauty.

Women did not start to recover any lost ground until the 19th century. Shlain believes this is due to the introduction of photography, a visual art. Photography shifted the culture from the written word back to the image. It is during this time in history that we see a rise in women's rights and an actual organized women's rights movement. Large numbers of women suddenly refused to tolerate the injustices that had long been perpetuated against them.

The hold that the linear alphabet had held for millennia was beginning to lose its grip. In 1854 the Catholic Church declared that Mary had not been conceived in Original Sin. She ceased to be a mortal at that point. This was also a time of intense religious feelings and women were at the forefront. Mary Baker Eddy founded Christian Science and Helena Blavatsky founded Theosophy. Also many Eastern mystical traditions that espoused a balance of masculine and feminine principles (Sufism, Kabbalah, astrology) were becoming popular in the West and Europe.

The next invention that helped promote right brained activity was the television. Television with its images in every home has pulled people together into a global community. Watching television generates slow alpha and theta waves, which denote a passive and contemplative state of mind. Reading a book generates beta waves, which appear whenever someone is concentrating on a task. PET scans have shown that reading generates left brain activity and watching television generates right brain activity.

The newest development that reinforces right brain perceptions is the computer, with its images and icons, words are hardly necessary. The computer is an interactive television. This had further diminished male dominance. Television and computers have had a greater impact in the last 50 years than the printing presses have in the last 500. This has also had impact on signs in public. They all show icons or images instead of words just like the sign on the restroom door.

In summary, alphabets in this theory are the principal reason that the Goddess was reviled, women banned from conducting religious ceremonies and nature devalued. The women who suffered these indignities were not always aware they suffered because they too fell under the spell of literacy. Only because we are recently shifting to a new paradigm of communication have we begun to realize the alphabet's role in the repression of women. Due to the alphabet's overwhelming benefits its side effects have been overlooked.

The last major theory on the reason for the shift to patriarchy was a necessary psychological and evolutionary step. It was necessary for man to separate himself from nature or the Goddess so that he could develop a separate consciousness or ego and heal the separation between our animal and human natures. When man realizes that he is a creature that is separate from other plants and animals it creates a psychological wound because he has thought of the Goddess as everything. Man must be either part of this wholeness or realize that he is different and no longer a part of the whole. The only way for man to develop was to pull away from the Goddess as a son must leave his mother's home or he would cease to grow.

The unconscious psyche can be described as the "feminine" principle in the mind and the ego is seen as more masculine. The unconscious is our psychic ground with the universe; it is intuitive and creative and has limitless power potential. The ego is more logical and concerned with maintaining its control. Based on this information, then it was necessary for the ego to develop. But now the ego has suppressed the feminine for such a long time it has become neurotic and needs to recognize the unconscious and its power before it destroys itself and the world.

Owen Barfield argued that human consciousness needed to detach itself from participation with nature, in order to gain more space, more play between this world and itself. Then consciousness could expand and learn to name and control outward phenomena. Divinity is then drawn away from nature and the loss of numinous power in things that can be felt is freer to shape its surroundings. Of course this later turns into abuse and domination without the feminine to keep it in check.

Out of the above theories for the reason for the shift to patriarchy, all three play a role in the new paradigm from Goddess to God. The invasion from warrior tribes would have the greatest effect; since those who opposed the invaders were sacrificed there would be no dissenters to continue Goddess worship. The effects of literacy are an interesting theory and it probably had an effect but not the far ranging effects seen in and of itself. The need for ego development probably had some minimal effect but it would have occurred before Neolithic times and not during the Iron Age. By then most of humankind would have been able to distinguish themselves from other animals.

RE-EMGERGENCE OF THE GODDESS TODAY

Throughout the world today there are numerous traditions of Goddess worship that have claimed to flourish unbroken to the present day. In India, Native Americans, Southeast Asia, Tibet and Africa the Goddess is still revered. Within Wicca and Neo-Paganism the Goddess is still worshipped. In Catholic countries the Goddess is worshipped through the Saints or the Virgin Mary.

In India today, the Goddess Kali is still worshipped, however the sacrifices are that of animals. Also there are manifestations or reincarnations of the divine mother that are worshipped. In her book *The Path of the Mother* (2000), Savirtri Bess worshiped at an ashram for a woman named Ammachi, who is known locally as reincarnation of the Divine Mother. Ammachi teaches her followers through meditation to love her and through her love everyone else. She teaches selfless service and living without pride. She also teaches how to deal with shadow issues and sublimate the ego. These are all very Eastern ideas for a Mother Goddess.

In her book, *The Altar of my Soul* (2000), Marta Vega describes what it was like to become a Yoruba priestess in the Santeria tradition. Santeria honors the divine essence of nature through the worship of Saints. It provides the means to live in the sacred moment and benefit from divine energy. Each of the Orishas or Gods and Goddesses represent an aspect of nature's energy. Santeria originated in Nigeria as the Yoruba religion. Since the worship of the Orishas was not allowed when the Africans came to the New World as slaves, the Orishas were given names of various saints, which did not offend their new masters. Every element is positive and negative. There are a total of 401 Orishas but only 11 are commonly worshipped. The most common are:

Obatala	God of Creation (Virgin Mary)
Yemaya	Goddess of Oceans (Our Lady of Regla)
Ellegua	God of Messages and Crossroads (St. Anthony)
Oyo	Goddess of Wind and Storms (St. Therese)
Shango	God of Thunder and Lightning (St. Barbara)
Ochun	Goddess of Fresh Water (La Caridad del Cobre)

Ochosi	God of Hunt (St. Norbert)
Oggun	God of Truth and Iron (St. Peter)
Aganyu	God of Volcanoes (St. Christopher)
Orunla	God of Divination (St. Francis)
Babalu	God of Healing (St. Lazarus)

Santeria is practiced today in the United States among Hispanics and in Latin America countries in South and Central America. Each Orisha has a positive and negative side so they can be used for good or evil. Their rituals often demand animal sacrifice. Remnants of the original mother Goddess can be seen in some of the Orishas.

Curanderismo is a combination of Aztec Gods and Goddesses and Catholicism. Curanderismo is a religion in which medicine and spirituality are practiced together. A Curandero is a healer. Most Curanderos are from Mexico. On their altars can be seen statues of the Virgin Mary, Jesus and some Aztec Goddesses. Curanderos invoke the healing powers of the Gods and Goddesses on behalf of the patients.

Probably the largest groups of modern Goddess worshippers are the Wiccans and Neo-Pagans. This vast international network can trace its origins back to the ancient traditions of Egypt, Mesopotamia, Greece, India and North America. The majority of pagans are middle-class people living in the Western world drawn by paganism's holistic message, which emphasizes the oneness of humankind with Nature and its accent on freedom of belief and religious practice. In the early 1990s there were some 100, 000 pagans in the United States (Husain, 1997).

The two basic books seen as an introduction to Neo-paganism, Wicca and Goddess spirituality are *Drawing Down the Moon* by Margot Adler and *The Spiral Dance* by Starhawk. Both books were originally published in 1979. Margot Adler said the following about Neo-paganism,

> The world is holy. Nature is holy. The body is holy. Sexuality is holy. The mind is holy. The imagination is holy. You are holy. A spiritual path that is not stagnant ultimately leads one to the understanding of one's own divine nature. Thou are Goddess. Thou are God. Divinity is imminent in all Nature. It is as much within you as without.
>
> In our culture which as for so long denied and denigrated the feminine as negative, evil or, at best, small and unimportant, women (and men too) will never understand their own creative strength and divine nature until they embrace the creative feminine, the source of inspiration, the Goddess within.
>
> While one can at times be cut off from experiencing the deep and ever-present connection between oneself and the universe, there is no such thing as sin (unless it is simply defined as that estrangement) and guilt is never very useful.
>
> The energy you put into the world comes back.

Neo-pagans and Wiccans share the goal of living in harmony with nature and they see ritual as a tool to end the current alienation with nature. Magic is often used to meet their goals. Magic is described as a collection of techniques, all of which involve the mind. These techniques include the mobilization of confidence, will and emotion brought about by the recognition of necessity; the use of imaginative faculties, particularly the ability to visualize, in order to begin to understand how other beings function in nature so we can use this knowledge to achieve necessary goals.

Pagans are defined as members of polytheistic nature religions such as ancient Greek, Roman or Egyptian or indigenous folk and tribal religions all over the world. Wiccans find their inspiration from pre-Christian sources, European mythology and folklore.

They both consider themselves priests and priestesses of an ancient European shamanistic nature religion that worships a Goddess who is related to the ancient Mother Goddess in her three aspects as Maiden, Mother, and Crone. Many craft traditions also worship a God related to the ancient horned lord of the animals, God of the hunt, of death and forests. Most Wiccans and Neo-Pagans observe seasonal rites and festivals and the lunar cycles.

As in ancient times, the priest and priestess function as the God and Goddess incarnate. The three central beliefs of this new generation of Goddess worshippers are polytheism (the many aspects of Nature are seen as emanating from the same divine force), pantheism (the Goddess' presence in Nature leads to its deification), and animism (objects as well as plants and animals are perceived to possess the universal life-energy which binds everything).

As the likeness of the Goddess, Pantheism has given a fresh new way of viewing the female body. Women are once again considered containers of the divine and their bodies are worthy of veneration. This perception has given females a self-esteem boost. The Goddess is also seen as immanent. She is not separate from the world, she is the world. She does not rule the world, she is the world.

Since the decline of the Goddess religions thousands of years ago, women have lacked religious models and spiritual systems that speak to female needs and experience. Large numbers of women have been seeking a spiritual framework outside the patriarchal religions that have dominated the Western world for the last several thousand years. Many who wanted to find a spiritual side to their feminism entered the Craft because of its Goddess worship. Many in the Craft see it as a way to turn humanity away from its destructive nature.

Many are drawn to the craft due to its freedom and lack of dogma. Their only ethic can be seen in an often quoted phrase called the Wiccan creed "An ye harm none, do what ye will." Since most Wiccans believe in karma and reincarnation another oft quoted law is the Threefold Law, "whatever you do returns to you times three".

Some of the famous 20th century founding fathers and mothers of the Neo-Pagans and Wiccans are Doreen Valiente, Zsusanna Budapest, Gerald Gardner, Aidan Kelly, Aleister Crowley, Rosemary and Ray Buckland of Gardnerian Tradition, Alex Sanders of Alexandrian Tradition, and Stewart and Janet Farrar. Many Wiccans still face persecution because Wicca is not recognized as a religion by most people and governments.

In *The Charge of the Goddess,* another often quoted and re-written verse, the ancient rituals of the Goddess can be seen. The following is adapted by Starhawk (1999):

> Listen to the words of the Great Mother, who of old was called Artemis, Astarte, Dione, Melusine, Aphrodite, Ceridwen, Diana, Arionrhod, Brigid, and by many other names:
> "Whenever you have need of anything, once in the month and better it be when the moon is full, you shall assemble in some secret place and adore the spirit of Me who is Queen of all the Wise. You shall be free from slavery and as a sigh that you be free you shall be naked in all your rites. Sing, feast, dance, make music and love, all in My presence, for Mine is the ecstasy of the spirit and Mine also is joy on earth. For My law is love unto all beings. Mine is the secret that opens upon the door of youth, and Mine is the cup of wine of life that is the Cauldron of Ceridwen that is the holy grail of immortality. I give the knowledge of the spirit eternal and beyond death I give peace and freedom and reunion with those that have gone before. Nor do I demand aught of sacrifice, for behold, I am the mother of all things and My love is poured upon the earth."

> Hear the words of the Star Goddess, the dust of
> whose feet are the hosts of heaven, whose body encircles
> the universe:
> "I who am the beauty of the green earth and the
> white moon among the stars and the mysteries of the
> waters, I call upon your soul to arise and come unto me.
> For I am the soul of nature that gives life to the universe.
> From Me all things proceed and unto Me they must return.
> Let My worship be in the heart that rejoices, for behold –
> all acts of love and pleasure are My rituals. Let there be
> beauty and strength, power and compassion, honor and
> humility, mirth and reverence within you. And you who
> seek to know Me, know that your seeking and yearning will
> avail you not, unless you know the Mystery: for if that
> which you seek, you find not within yourself, you will
> never find it without. For behold, I have been with you
> from the beginning and I am that which is attained at the
> end of desire."

The quote from above shows a direct link with Goddess worship in ancient times. The same loving, Mother Goddess is once again being worshipped and experienced on a personal basis. The Charge of the Goddess reflects the Craft understanding of the Goddess. The list of Goddess names are not seen as separate beings but as different aspects of the same being that is all beings. Different Goddess names will be used for different reasons and at different times of the year during rituals.

Need refers to spiritual and physical needs. The full moon meetings honor the Goddess at the height of her power, when the tides are strongest. Slavery originally meant that all were equal in the circle regardless of social position but today there is also mental and emotional slavery. Nakedness represents truth. Rituals are fun and pleasurable. Love is the law of the Goddess, whether it is passionate love, platonic love or motherly love. The secret of immortality lies in seeing death as an integral art of the cycle of life. The Goddess is the symbol of the innermost self for women. For men the Goddess is his hidden female self. All phases of life are sacred and age is seen as a blessing and not a curse.

The God in witchcraft is called the Horned God. He is very different from any stereotype in our culture. He is neither macho nor effeminate. He is gentle, tender and comforting, but he is also the Hunter. He is the Dying God, but his death is always in the service of the life force. He is untamed sexuality – as a deep, holy and connecting power. He is the feeling of power, the image of what men could be if they were liberated from the constraints of patriarchal culture (Starhawk, 1999).

The image of the Pagan God has been deliberately distorted by the medieval Church into the image of the Christian Devil. Witches do not believe in nor do they worship the Devil, it is a Christian concept. The God is depicted as wearing horns because they are the waxing and waning crescents of the Goddess Moon and his symbol of animal vitality and his wild nature.

The God is the modern version of the Son-lover of the Goddess. He is born of the Virgin Goddess at the Winter Solstice. His rituals follow the pattern of the sun or the Wheel of the Year (seasons). Her rituals follow the moon. On May Day he is fully matured and marries (Sacred Marriage) the Goddess. He dies and is mourned on August 1 during harvest. He returns to the womb of the Goddess to be reborn on the next Winter Solstice.

The practices of Native North Americans have had a major influence on Goddess movements in the United States. Modern Native Americans of the Santa Clara Pueblo perform an annual corn dance, which is intended to promote the fertility of the earth and encourage the growth of corn. The corn maidens who encourage growth of crops must be persuaded to return annually through this ritual.

The Changing Woman of the Navajo and Apache Native Americans is a Nature deity who brought light to the earth. She is also known as the Mother of All who emerges from the four doors of her heavenly home to create the seasons. She rises with the spring flowers, matures with the summer, ages with the autumn and goes to sleep with the winter (Husain, 1997). Changing woman represents all the phases of the female, but most particularly the moment when a girl becomes a woman. This transition is believed to be beneficial to the entire tribe and it is marked by feasting and ritual. Changing Woman created the Navajo ancestors and taught them to live in harmony with nature. Most Native American rituals have changed little since ancient times.

Another modern but pale version of the Goddess is the Virgin Mary. She is not a Goddess in the truest sense and her powers are restricted by the patriarchal Church but she is still venerated by many. Her veneration is certainly not justified by the Bible where she plays a minor role as the vessel, which contained the Savior. Her popularity speaks of a deep need for a connection with the divine feminine.

Mary was depicted as docile, guiltless and innocent of sexual experience in order to meet the Jewish criteria of womanly goodness. This eradicated her dark side as is seen in most depictions of the divine feminine and creates a dualism. Still Mary was given many pagan attributes and miracles, which endeared her to the masses.

Today she performs blessings and inspires mass pilgrimages and commands her own body of worship. She is seen as humankind's intercessor with God. Statues and portraits of the Virgin Mary were thought to have great healing powers and still do today.

There are many reports of weeping statues of the Virgin Mary and not all of them are in churches, for example the weeping statue of Our Lady at Maasmechelen, Belgium. In Santiago, Chile in 1992 a small statuette was shedding blood. The local coroner's office determined that it was type-O human blood. These events draw many worshippers to the cult of Mary, much as they would have in ancient times. The Virgin Mary may not be exactly the Great Goddess of ancient times but in our collective unconscious she is the Christian successor.

One topic, which has not been discussed, is the advent of Feminism, which can be seen as a direct result of the stirring of the Goddess, a call to right what has been wrong for so many years.

Only in recent years, relatively speaking, have women been able to voice their frustrations about a patriarchal and vengeful God. In colonial times, this type of heresy was grounds for hanging or burning as a witch. In the 1830s Sarah and Angelina Grimke demanded their God-given rights to participate in the abolition movement along with their fellow male Quakers. They were constrained by religious ideas about the inferiority of women and the laws of the times.

Elizabeth Stanton and Susan Anthony led the women's suffrage movement in the late 1800s. They gathered a small group of female Theosophists, Freethinkers and New Thought leaders that wrote the Declaration of Sentiments and *The Woman's Bible.* The Declaration of Sentiments was based on the Declaration of Independence and voiced 12 grievances whereby women's freedom was curtailed by men (Borysenko, 1999). They included the fact that women had no legal rights, no vote, divorce and custody laws were entirely in favor of men and women were barred from universities and professions like medicine and law. *The Woman's Bible* pointed out some of the abuses of women in The Bible.

In 1920 women got the vote. Then during World War II women worked in the factories in traditional men's jobs. It was difficult for them to return to their kitchens after the war ended thus the Civil Rights and Women's Movements of the 1960's and 1970's were born.

Things are radically different today and it is difficult to imagine that they have not always been this way. More progress is still needed such as parity in the workplace, equality in intimate relationships, non-gender based education for children, the re-writing of history by a sisterhood and re-writing of language. In spite of all the progress, too many women are still angry at men, patriarchy and traditional religions. As stated in *The Woman's Bible* "We rise and fall together." It is time to move forward to a time of cooperation.

EFFECTS OF THE RE-EMERGENCE OF THE DIVINE FEMININE

We are currently witnessing a reawakening of the feminine, an upheaval within the consciousness of women. Some men fear it, some are challenged by it. All the assumptions and values women have about themselves, politics, sexual relationships, and their place in the universe are being challenged. It is time to develop a new psychology of the feminine that returns women to their roots (Woolger, 1989).

Some of the outward signs of this emergence are feminism, birth control, better health care, and opening of the urban marketplace to women, freer divorce laws, women's suffrage, growing demands for women as ministers and shifting attitudes towards sexuality.

There are three categories of effects, which will be discussed in relation to the re-emergence of the divine feminine. These are psychological, spiritual or religious and evolutionary. All three are interconnected.

Psychological Effects

As Jung said, "Nothing in the psyche is ever lost". Issues fall into the unconscious where they continue to influence the conscious psyche. There must be a dialogue held in full consciousness in order to dispel these issues. The issues here are the damage that has been done by a society that has ignored or denigrated the feminine.

The rediscovery of the ancient Goddess civilizations has given us a deep sense of pride in woman's ability to create and sustain culture. It has exposed the falsehoods of patriarchal history and given us models of female strength and authority. Once again we recognize the Goddess. She is the bridge to which we can reconnect with our lost potentials. We can explore our inner selves.

Western humankind must arrive at a synthesis that includes the feminine. Only then can we hope to achieve psychic wholeness, which is urgently needed if man is to face the dangers that threaten his existence. In analytical psychology, when the archetype of the Great Mother is referred to, it is an image in the human psyche. It is the symbolic expression of this Great Goddess that can be found in myths and artistic creations that are a true expression of the unconscious where she has been buried for so long. The dynamic of the archetype takes hold of the entire personality. It extends beyond the unconscious and exerts influence on the mood, inclinations and tendencies of the personality and ultimately on its conceptions, intentions, interests and conscious direction of the mind (Neumann, 1974).

The internal symbol or image of the archetype impels the psyche to assimilate the unconscious content of the symbol. This assimilation culminates in the formation of views, orientations and concepts of consciousness. One essential feature of the primordial archetype is that it contains both positive and negative attributes. Early humans interpreted this paradox as unity in the godhead. When consciousness developed they came to be worshipped as separate deities.

In early humans, life was determined to a higher degree by the unconscious than consciousness. Behavior was directed more by archetypal images than by the ego. Humans were more part of a group than individuals.

One of the early symbols of the Goddess was the uroboros or the circular snake biting its tail. This is symbolic of the original situation in which the consciousness and the ego were still small and undeveloped.

Neumann divides the Feminine into two essential parts, the elementary and the transformative. The elementary is the aspect of the Feminine as the Great Round or Great Container which holds fast to everything that springs forth from it and surrounds it like an eternal substance. This has been associated with the matriarchy and the early consciousness of humans when the ego was still small and undeveloped and the unconscious was dominant. In the transformative character of the Feminine, the accent is on the dynamic element of the psyche, which drives toward motion, change, and of course transformation. The transformative stage develops from the elementary stage and assumes its own independent form.

When the elementary form is dominant all processes of change take place within the unconscious. In the transformative stage the personality is differentiated (anima). It brings movement and unrest. Each stage has positive and negative imagery to illustrate his theory of the archetypal Feminine, Neumann has drawn a circle with four polar points on it labeled The Good Mother (positive elementary), the Bad Mother (negative elementary), the negative anima (seductive young witch or negative transformative character) and the positive anima (Sophia – Virgin or positive transformative character).

The positive elementary character of the Feminine can be seen in the ancient symbolism of a vessel or jar, a figure of a many-breasted mother, mother-child nursing, Isis-Horus and the making of clay pots which was mostly done by women in the ancient days. The negative character of the Feminine can be seen in the growing struggle between maternal-feminine and male child as he develops and tries to break away from the Mother. The Terrible Mother represents the black, abysmal side of life and the human psyche. It is disease, hunger, hardship. They are symbolized in the Goddesses Kali and Durga as Guardians of the Dead.

The unconscious has become associated with the feminine and the conscious has become associated with the masculine. The Great Goddess is the incarnation of the Feminine self that unfolds in the history of mankind and in history of every individual woman. It determines individual as well as collective life.

The stereotyped notions of masculine and feminine have had a constricting and inhibiting effect on development. The psychological effects of the return of the Goddess are mostly developmental but some have had therapeutical effects as well. The Goddess in her many aspects gives women new role models to follow: she can be a nurturing mother, a playful child, an old wise woman, a lover, an intellectual or business woman, warrior and a wife.

Women tend to be overinhibited in the direct expression of anger and aggression (Lerner, 1988). The Goddesses such as Kali and Durga will help them to express that anger in creative ways and learn that it is acceptable to have those emotions.

Spiritual or Religious Effects

Women's spiritual groups are cropping up everywhere, not just in the New Age circles but also in traditional religions. Women of color, gay and straight, feminists and nonfeminists are seeking an authentic spirituality. God as a jealous, punitive white Anglo-Saxon male with a long beard lacks appeal for many women today. This has led women to join Neo-Pagan and Buddhist groups where there is no personified God.

More of the traditional religions are allowing women to become ministers. For eons women have been viewed as second-class citizens by the three main patriarchal religions, Judaism, Christianity and Islam, but if you attend a service, especially Christian you will usually see more women present than men. It speaks of a deep spiritual need in women.

If women's needs are not met the biggest threat to patriarchal religion is not attack by women but women leaving them behind. The worship of the Virgin Mary and her different aspects and incarnations around the world has helped some women to remain in traditional religions such as Catholicism. In Mary, women can see a nurturing, compassionate intercessor, who they can communicate with directly.

The religious words and images of a Father God, of judgment and punishment, of unworthiness and shame remain in women's unconscious. Whether you were raised in a religious family or not the pervasive influence of religion in our formative years cannot be discounted. No matter how much you distance yourself you still carry your religious past with you on whatever new spiritual path you choose as an adult. In her book, *A God Who Looks Like Me,* Patricia Reilly (1995) provides a clear overview of the religious baggage women bring with them into adulthood. She offers a practical guide for sorting through this baggage and advises women to discard what is harmful and use what is woman-affirming. This will be discussed in more detail in the section on Therapeutical Interventions.

Effects on Evolution

Humans are rapidly approaching an evolutionary crossroads. Our choice at this crossroad is critical. Of all life forms on this planet, only humans can plant crops, create music, enjoy lovemaking and express emotion. Because of the technologies we have created, we are also the only species that has the capability to destroy ourselves and all life on this planet. Since going back is not the answer, how do we move forward? A major cultural evolution will be necessary.

For millennia men have fought wars but this does not mean that men are inevitably violent and warlike. Throughout history there have been peaceful and nonviolent men. The root of the problem is in the social system that teaches men and women to equate true masculinity with violence and dominance and men who do not conform to this ideal as soft and effeminate (Eisler, 1987).

What Eisler proposes is a partnership model of society as opposed to the current dominator model. A partnership model is based on the principle of linking as opposed to ranking. They tend to be more peaceful and less hierarchal and authoritarian. Dominator models are based on either patriarchies or matriarchies.

All modern, post-Enlightenment movements for social justice such as feminist, peace and ecology movements can be seen as an underlying push towards transformation to a partnership model of society. It is our species evolutionary thrust for survival. Dominator societies threaten life on our planet and are maladaptive.

There are times throughout the history of humankind that allow for changes in society. Opportunities when feminine ideals are awarded some importance. These are chances to take a different direction in our evolution. For example in the Middle Ages in France; chivalry was popular and the Virgin Mary had many worshippers. Unfortunately the movement did not survive as not enough people supported it. Now we are coming to another "bifurcation" or branch in our evolution in which we can choose to continue with a system that leads to eventual destruction of ourselves and our planet or to choose a different path. All is not hopeless as long as we recognize that it is not human nature but a dominator society that drives us to nuclear war and destruction of our planet.

Some of the recent historical events that have started us down a path away from dominator societies and towards partnership societies have been the American and French Revolutions, which were based on freedom and equality and secular ideologies such as capitalism, socialism, communism and feminism.

Evolution is not predetermined; we can create our future. A partnership society offers us a viable alternative. This global partnership also allows us to reexamine the roles of women and men in our society. One way to facilitate this transformation is to recognize that humans have a higher need for growth or actualization than other animals.

A shift from defense needs to actualization needs is the key to the transformation from a dominator to a partnership society (Eisler, 1987).

Leonard Shlain in his book, *The Alphabet Versus the Goddess,* theorizes that the downfall of the Goddess was caused by the advent of writing. That writing caused the growth and dominance of left brain thinking, which manifested as Gods replacing the Goddess with a warrior society. He proposes that we are entering a new age, which will tend back towards equilibrium.

If we are indeed entering a new age as all factors point to, then perhaps we are also entering a new stage in our evolutionary growth. If the underdeveloped left hemisphere received a tremendous growth spurt as a result of writing then what may happen when equilibrium is achieved? It is possible that humans will develop a new lobe from the synthesis of the right and left hemisphere or perhaps a larger, stronger corpus callosum. What might this new brain area do? Instead of communication through images or through words, perhaps direct communication mind to mind? It is possible and probable. Some humans already posses this trait to a small degree. We are indeed on the brink of a new age.

REVIEW OF RESEARCH PROJECT

The empirical study that preceded this paper was a correlational study between the Keirsey Temperament Sorter and God/Goddess Archetypes. The entire study is included in Appendix A. The study was meant to show a correlation between the outcome of the Keirsey and the outcome of the Archetype test.

Unfortunately, 61% could not select the appropriate archetype for their personality type. This may be due to the inadequate descriptions of the archetypes. Those with more introspective personality did have a higher rate of selecting the correct archetype.

Since there are four main categories of personalities (Guardians, Idealists, Artisans and Rationals), four Gods and four Goddesses that fit those personality types were utilized in the archetype test. Many of the subjects enjoyed the test according to the feedback received and were really more interested in the archetypes than the Myers-Briggs Jungian personality types. They seemed to like the idea of having an image to connect to a personality type as opposed to initials (ENTJ).

Further research for this somewhat related paper indicates that perhaps the Jungian personality types are not appropriate at all. Several of the participants felt that their assigned type did not fit them at all so the test was administered a second time. The results of the second test indicated a completely different type. This indicates that perhaps personality is more fluid, depending on the environment in which you take the test and what may be happening in your life at that particular moment.

Further research indicates that there are many Gods and Goddesses in each man and woman. There is not just one. Usually only one is dominate at any particular time or moment. Others can be called on if their strengths are needed.

The Jungian perspective indicates that women (and men) are influenced by powerful inner forces, archetypes, which can be personified by Goddesses (or Gods). Stereotypes enforced by a patriarchal society which expects women (and men) to conform – reinforce some Goddess (or God) and repress others. Relationship patterns also show the imprint of particular Goddesses (or Gods) such as father-daughter, mother-daughter and lover-lover. Jung's types are inadequate to explain all situations.

The Goddess archetypes provide an explanation for inconsistencies between women's behavior and Jung's theory of psychological types. For example a person is supposed to be either introverted or extraverted in attitude; to use feeling or thinking as an assessing mode; and perceive through either intuition or sensation. The Goddess archetypes provide an explanation for the exceptions in women.

A woman can shift from one facet of herself to another, she can be an Athena oriented business woman at work and a Hera house-keeper at home. This bridges the gaps that a many-sided woman has in determining her Jungian type. Clinically speaking the Goddess archetypes have the ability to overwhelm the ego for conscious control when they have been ignored or subsumed by other archetypes for too long. This can cause psychiatric symptoms for those who are unable to integrate the needs of the different archetypes or subpersonalities. The client must decide which Goddess is to express herself and when and how. Each Goddess has positive and negative characteristics and some are antagonistic to the others.

These archetypes were once all part of the Great Goddess but have been fragmented over time. Archetypes are patterns of instinctual behavior that are contained in the collective unconscious. The Great Goddess still exists in the collective unconscious and is demanding attention after being silenced for so many millennia.

The Goddesses are potential patterns in the psyches of all women, some are activated and some are not. These patterns can be activated for different reasons – inherent predisposition, family environment, culture, stage of life, hormones and people and events (Bolen, 1984). The next section on therapeutic interventions will discuss how this can be utilized for growth.

THERAPEUTIC INTERVENTIONS

Thousands of years of patriarchal rule have left both women and men wounded. Slowly we are awakening to the re-emergence of the Goddess. She is pushing up from the unconscious and demanding that we acknowledge her and her symbolism. We can see this in the many changes as discussed earlier such as women's rights and better health care. It can also be seen in the growing demand for female ministers. All these changes reflect unprecedented changes in the deeper psychic structures that underlie our culture.

Another example is our shifting attitudes towards sexuality, which will be discussed in detail later in this section. These changes in the last hundred years include Freudianism, free love, open marriage, pornography, easy divorce, and gay and lesbian marriages.

These longings that lead us to question our religions and institutions are not imposed from outside, they are stirrings felt so powerfully that they can only have internal origins. These inner pressures will eventually lead to social and political movements.

Themes taken up by novelists, movie script writers and artists reflect radically new images of the feminine bursting into the consciousness. This is a time of change and confusion for all involved until equilibrium has been established. Women and men are discovering new roles. For some time to come male and female interactions will be difficult.

Both sexes must struggle to integrate these new roles into their traditional roles. They must both find their way on a path that has not been traveled before. These new adjustments will cause some psychological problems and some issues with growth and integration. Therapeutic interventions for assisting them on their journey will be discussed.

In the psychological context, a Goddess is a psychological description of a complex female character type that we intuitively recognize in ourselves and those around us. There is a fundamental dynamic behind the behavior of each Goddess that makes her unique, in part socially acquired. In a group of people this dynamic is recognized as an archetype.

Jennifer and Roger Woolger developed a system of Goddess Psychology that utilizes Goddess archetypes taken from the Greek pantheon (Woolger, 1989). This is a system, which has a test to determine your dominant Goddesses and a wheel, which demonstrates the dynamics of the different archetypes. This system can be utilized for individual therapy for specific issues and for workshops for potential growth.

Woolger states that when a new Goddess energy emerges in your life, you will find that everything is in disarray. They often appear at important changes in your life. These Goddess myths are actually psychology couched in the poetic language of image and drama. Greek Goddesses are utilized because they are already familiar. (As was used in the research project).

Woolger's system raises the question of a whole psychospiritual imbalance in our culture. This imbalance is perceived as a disharmony between the masculine and the feminine. What is missing is the feminine dimension in our spiritual and psychological lives, what used to be called the Great Mother. The disharmony manifests as cultural neuroticism.

Woolger compares our culture to the children of a family who have suffered through a terrible divorce. The children now live with the father and are forbidden to even mention the mother's name or reminisce about the happy times spent with her. The Father Archetype has overshadowed the Mother archetype and we have committed serious damage to our individual and collective psyches.

There is little chance of restoring the Great Mother Goddess to her former primordial unified state and it is debatable whether modern consciousness is suited to her. The different aspects and specializations of the Goddess actually suit the complexity of our modern society. Once we can recognize which Goddesses are dominant in our lives we must attend to those Goddesses within us that are weak, neglected, wounded or we may suffer neuroticism if we are too one-sided.

For example a woman can get stuck being the mother of a family (Hera) by not working (neglects Athena) and never addressing her sexuality (ignoring Aphrodite) or her inner world (Persephone). A man may flee intellectual women (Athena), avoid motherly women (Demeter) or strong women (Hera) and seek only exciting sexual partners (Aphrodite).

The first step in healing the wounded Goddesses within you is to dialogue with them either in your own psyche or among friends. Also encourage the Goddesses to interact among themselves. This will create powerful opportunities for change.

Woolger developed a questionnaire to determine your dominant Goddesses and how the others rate in your psyche. The test and scoring sheet has been reproduced in Appendix B.

Woolger's system describes six Goddesses from the Greek pantheon. They are Hera, Athena, Aphrodite, Persephone, Artemis and Demeter. Descriptions of their areas of influence follow.

Athena is the Goddess of wisdom. She was born by bursting from her father's head (Zeus), instead of the traditional birthing from a mother. She was the patron Goddess of Athens. Athena rules all aspects of cities, urban life and civilized pursuits, which maintain the city-state such as politics and law. She also rules technology, science, crafts, literary arts, education and intellectual life. Athena guides your career as it relates to the patriarchal world. An Athena woman is concerned with achievement, career, education, intellectual culture, social justice and politics.

Aphrodite is the Goddess of Love and Beauty. She was born from the foam in the sea. She encourages love between humans and between animals. Only a handful of the other Goddesses can resist her influence. Aphrodite rules all aspects of sexuality, intimacy and personal relationships. Since she has the power to entice and attract the senses, she is also Goddess of beauty, which includes not only humans but visual arts such as painting, sculpting, architecture, poetry and music. Her influence is private and individual rather than public and collective. She rules all creative liaisons between the sexes. To the Aphrodite woman, her chief concerns are relationships, sexuality, intrigue, romance, beauty and the inspiration of the arts.

Persephone is the Goddess of the Underworld. She is also the daughter of Demeter, Earth Mother. Persephone is usually depicted as a maiden. Her mythology tells her story of being kidnapped by Hades and taken to the Underworld where she must return yearly because she partook of food while held there. Persephone rules over all aspects of the spirit world or the realm of the dead. She is in contact with the greater transpersonal powers of the psyche archetypes by Jung. In psychological terms she rules over the deeper unconscious mind, dreams, paranormal phenomena and mysticism. She is concerned with mediumship, channeling, visions, occult matters and psychic healing. She will also be involved anytime there is a death or trauma. The Persephone woman is attracted to the spirit world, the occult and mystical experiences.

Artemis is the Goddess of Nature, the Moon and the Hunt. She is the daughter of Zeus and Leto. Her brother is Apollo. She is depicted wearing a short tunic and carrying a bow. She is usually accompanied by a stag or hunting dogs. Artemis is Goddess of nature in its virgin or untamed form. She is in contrast to Athena who stands for civilized and tamed nature. Artemis is especially close to animals and the hunt and those cycles of nature that rule animals and humans. She is also a Goddess of childbirth as she assisted in the delivery of her twin Apollo. Since she is also a Moon Goddess she rules over all instinctual life, which emphasizes the body as opposed to the mind. She lives for all physical and outdoor activities, which include athletics and dance. In nature she rules over hunting, killing and blood sacrifice. She complements and aids Persephone in regard to death: Artemis the death of the body and Persephone the passage of the spirit. An

Artemis woman is practical, athletic, and adventurous, likes physical culture, solitude, the outdoors, animals and is concerned with the environment, alternative life-styles and women's communities or feminism.

Demeter is the ancient Earth Mother Goddess who rules over crops and fertility of earth, animals and humans. Demeter rules everything connected with the reproductive functions – menstrual cycle and childbearing cycles. She also rules the seeds and fruit so she is also called the Lady of the Plants. She has a deep connection to crop cycles and harvesting and preserving. She is also concerned with the nurturing and caring for the growth of the body within children and infants and all growing creatures. The Demeter woman loves bearing, nurturing and raising children.

Lastly, Hera is the Queen of Heaven and Goddess of Marriage. She is concerned with power and rulership. As wife of Zeus, she rules over marriage, partnership and all public roles where a woman has power, responsibility or leadership. She is concerned with social morality and upholding the integrity of the family. She oversees all aspects of tradition and the cohesiveness of the community. She shares Athena's view of civilized life and the maintenance of patriarchal values symbolized by her husband Zeus. If her power is restricted to the family arena she becomes the matriarch. A Hera woman is concerned with marriage, partnerships with men and power.

Men are also influenced by Goddess archetypes. The Goddesses mirror feminine energies in the male psyche, which men usually experience as external to themselves in the shape of women they are attracted to or have strong relationships with. Men experience the Goddess projected onto the women around them. A man may unconsciously look for a Demeter woman or an Aphrodite girlfriend.

Woolger arranged the six Goddesses described above in dyads of introverted and extraverted and under similar descriptions of independence, power and love.

	Independence	Power	Love
Extraverted	Athena	Hera	Aphrodite
Introverted	Artemis	Persephone	Demeter

So in viewing the chart, you can see that Athena and Artemis are both independent, also they both carry weapons and neither has a mate. They are both the Virgin Goddesses in that they have no mates. Athena is more extraverted and Artemis is introverted. Since they are so closely related they are often seen in same woman.

Both Hera and Persephone are concerned with control of their worlds as Queen of Heaven and Queen of the Underworld. Hera as an extravert concerns herself with the outer world whereas Persephone concerns herself with the inner psychic realm. Hera's ego is extremely strong whereas Persephone's ego is weak in order to commune with her spirits.

The remaining pair of opposites is Demeter and Aphrodite. They are both concerned with love in some way. Demeter lovers her children and serves as a selfless container for all her children both physically and spiritually. Aphrodite nurtures spiritually and physically, but not to children. She gives her lover her full maturity; she loves the adult as opposed to the child. Demeter's love is more introverted and Aphrodite's love is more extraverted. For Demeter, her body is sacred vessel, for Aphrodite her body is a sacred love object.

All of this is demonstrated in the Goddess Wheel developed by the Woolgers. It has been reproduced in Appendix C. The Goddesses also have patterns as to how they relate to the opposite sex or their animus. The following describes how she will be attracted to or repelled by certain kinds of men.

Athena is drawn to men as heroic companions in arms with whom she can share ideals, ambitions and career goals and struggles. This is usually an intellectual companion or a rival. She will not usually marry them. She is also drawn to father figures. Her main animus counterparts are the companion hero and the father.

Aphrodite admires virility in a man as a lover or a warrior. She admires success and combativeness in her men but doesn't' want to fight with them. She is happy with multiple relationships and extramarital affairs. She also attracts creative men and often acts as a patroness to them.

Persephone is drawn more to the spirit world than real men and usually has male spirit guides. Her deep and fatalistic involvement in the darker side means she may unwittingly attract destructive men and sometimes marry them. To protect herself she may pick a younger male with an underdeveloped ego that she can mother. Her type animus is best described as the son-lover.

Artemis is very independent and doesn't have much need for a man in her life. Occasionally she enjoys a companionable male who will work alongside her. Marriage is not usually a goal and sexually she can be quite shy. Her animus counterpart is a friend, companion and brother.

<u>Demeter</u> needs a man to support her. She is not really interested in sex or intellectual relationships. Her best mate is a reliable earth father. She has an irresistible urge to mother all the men around her. Her animus is best described as the son-hero.

<u>Hera</u> wants a man who will be her partner and share power with her equally. She prefers strong, successful men who are leaders. She considers a marriage a partnership. She will always seek a man for his worldly power or social prestige.

<u>Recognizing the Goddesses today and their Psychological Issues</u>

It is easy to recognize <u>Athena</u> in modern society because as an extravert she is very visible. She is intelligent and men are usually intimidated. Her concerns are worldly. She works alongside men in business. She admires heroism and stirs up patriotism in those around her.

Young Athenas master language quickly. They are competitive and argumentative as children. They love word games and excel in traditional subjects in school.

She is sexually shy and puts motherhood on the back burner. She identifies with the patriarchal father image. Athenas wear armor to protect them emotionally. What Athena needs most is warm, natural, physical mothering and attention to her bodily needs. She also needs unconditional love. She is almost completely cut off from the feminine. She has inherited the patriarchal fear of the Dark Mother's power and does not recognize it as part of herself.

Athena spends too much time in her head. She lacks emotional intensity and misses the experience of being in her body. She is split between a fragile inner maiden and a tough outer fighter. The more she covers up her vulnerable maiden the thicker her protective shield will be and the more unconscious she will be of it. Athena's wound is in her heart. She tends to drive those away who try to help her because she has no way of letting down her defenses. Therapies that would help Athena are bodywork, dance and massage. In order to grow Athena women should turn inward to rediscover their inner child and their mother. Some famous Athenas are Joan of Arc, Queen Elizabeth I, Eleanor of Aquitaine and Sojourner Truth.

The modern version of an Artemis woman can feel out of place today. She will not stand out strongly in the world and she's uncomfortable in the city. Her energy isn't intellectual, it's physical. She loves to be involved physically in the project of the moment. She will probably be casually dressed as opposed to Athena in a business suit.

Nature is the key for Artemis women. She belongs in the wild, hunting, following animal rhythms and moon cycles because she is slightly boyish and rugged. Artemis women would excel at occupations like marine biologists and nature photographers.

She usually outperforms men physically. Athena has no consort. She wants men around for shared physical endeavors but may prefer the company of women. For men it may be difficult to have a relationship with Artemis women because she may reject intimacy. She also has the fear of the Terrible Mother.

Artemis is the oldest of the Goddesses. She was part of the primordial hunting cultures and she was also called upon for childbirth. Young Artemis women do not usually excel in school because it is too boring for them. They would rather be physically active so they excel in sports. They love their freedom and have a difficult time in puberty when their freedom is curtailed and they are expected to be more feminine.

Artemis's wound is alienation. She needs to be physically in touch with the Earth. Many Artemis women grow up in the city and they are literally out of place. To cultivate

Artemis, cultivate solitude. She is on the fringe of society and is resentful that she does not get the attention of Aphrodite. Artemis must come to realize that both she and Aphrodite are living under false female stereotypes promoted by a patriarchal society. Artemis needs to become vulnerable and love and care deeply about another person. Her fierce love of freedom makes it difficult for her to accept the lifestyle of mother, wife or career woman.

Another of her issues is that she is androgynous; she already contains all the feminine and masculine attributes that the other Goddesses project onto men. As a Virgin Goddess she is self-sufficient and is complete within herself. When she is in touch with her true eros, her love play is wild and fierce. In the ancient cults of Artemis sexuality was uninhibited.

Today Artemis women will be seen involved in the Green Movement, Eco-feminism and the Gaia movement. They advocate a spiritual revolution and awakening of the Earth spirit. You will also see many Artemis women involved in Wicca and Native American traditions. One example of a modern Artemis is Jane Goodall.

Aphrodite, Goddess of Love and Beauty, is one of the most adored of the Goddesses. She was adored for her beauty, gentleness and her amorous adventures. Love was seen by the Greeks as being the divine force behind all living things.

In modern times it appears that Aphrodite has moved to Hollywood. She can be seen depicted as screen goddesses such as Greta Garbo, Marilyn Monroe and Elizabeth Taylor. Her influence can also be seen in television, romance novels, sex therapy talk shows, pornography and prostitution.

In ancient times Aphrodite was honored; sex was seen as a sacred gift and not a commodity to be exploited. Since then the influence of Christianity can be seen. They were horrified at Aphrodite's love of the body and sexual pleasure. For two thousand years we have learned to suppress sexual urges and now that the pendulum is swinging back everything is toward excess.

Aphrodite is sensual in all things. She has a natural appreciation of sexuality and beauty as sacred. She loves dresses, hair and jewelry. She is an exhibitionist and can be seen in models and actresses. She loves to be around groups of people. Relatedness is important to Aphrodite. She wants us to be fully present with her or she loses interest.

She has an instinctual warmth. She has a personal relationship with her mate and wants relationships to be amicable, social, physical and spiritual or from the heart. She doesn't care about a good marriage (Hera) or mother love (Demeter) or a meeting of minds (Athena).

She is civilized and sensual, and is not into backpacking; her adventures include cocktails and clean linens. She is so at ease with her sexuality she is considered a natural pagan.

To men she is seen as a flirt and an extravert. She is usually courted by older men. This develops into an inner loneliness because these men want her just for her good looks. Her attractiveness can set her apart from other women who become jealous cohorts. She is mysterious and exotic to men; they see her as a seductress, a siren. She will usually have affairs with married men and is often the other woman in love triangles.

Aphrodite helps men to develop their creative side. She is attracted to executives, tycoons, politicians and other powerful males. Aphrodite's open sexual behavior threatens patriarchal society where the lineage is passed down through the father. Aphrodite was suppressed by the Church, which resulted in a sexual neurosis.

None of the Goddesses has been abused more than Aphrodite by our patriarchal society. The other Goddesses have learned to accommodate patriarchy but this is not so with Aphrodite because they can't live without her but neither can they live with her so they have done everything possible to restrict and confine her. She is not really vindictive as she has been depicted but prefers to nurse her wounds quietly since she is profoundly forgiving.

Aphrodite's wounds stem from restrictions and abuse from the dominant patriarchal society and from the other Goddesses who disapprove of her. This society often treats her with hostility so she needs the strengths of the other Goddesses to thrive. She could use some of Athena's thinking ability in order to advance in a career and to think clearly when faced with unsuitable or manipulative mates. Hera could also help her to settle down.

Aphrodite women get caught between their desire for sexual connection and their ability to generate erotic energy in others. She lives in the present with no consideration for what consequences her actions may manifest in the future. Experience is her best teacher. Men can become casualties to her. She is sincerely convinced that each one of them is the "one". She must accept human flaws. She must see that love can also be destructive if he treats her badly and should let him go.

For women who are out of touch with Aphrodite in their lives, they need to be fully aware of and cherish their bodies. They need to explore touch. They need to do things, which enliven their senses – flowers, clothes on the skin, food or music. If we are able to open up to our senses and risk being vulnerable, Aphrodite will teach us tolerance and patience.

Hera, the Goddess of Marriage, is another Goddess that stands out in a crowd because she is usually the one in control. She is confident and is in command of herself and everyone around her. She usually manifests in an older woman. She is a natural authority figure, born to rule. She has an affinity for power, elitism and can be arrogant and intemperate. She thrives within the partnership of marriage.

Hera as the wife of a great man, Zeus, can be ruthless and is seen as a matriarch or queen bee. On the surface, Hera of today will have a successful marriage, grown children, a long family tradition and will usually be dressed conservatively. Love from her children is secondary to respect and honor. Family gatherings and big social events bring out the best in a Hera woman.

Hera was originally a Mother Goddess but was demoted to the status of an interfering wife in the Greek pantheon. She is married to Zeus who has unbounded promiscuity. He is the ultimate power of the Father World. This relationship is indicative of the forced merging of the peaceful Goddess culture with the patriarchal warrior tribes. Marriage then or now perpetuates the patriarchal supremacy. She is the embodiment of all that will make her mate complete so she shares in his power.

The Hera archetype does not fully manifest until the second half of life. On the surface she appears to be a young Athena as both are bright and self-confident. From her children she expects good behavior, neat rooms and obedience. From her husband she expects partnership and equality. She becomes deeply interested in his career. Intrigue and gossip fascinate her. If she marries a weak man she will manipulate him.

Hera's psychic wound is the fear of powerlessness. She is jealous of the freedom that her husband has to be a moving force in the world. If he does not let her participate, her self-esteem is deeply wounded and she will be resentful of him. In reaction she will possessively cling to her husband to vicariously experience his politics and demand that she be his advisor. Frustrated Heras will fall back on their families and can be harsh disciplinarians.

Hera constricts her life to her husband's interests. She has an idealized image of her husband. In order to grow, Hera needs to expand beyond herself and transform her rage and pain into creative outlets.

What Hera needs is to dialogue with Aphrodite. In Aphrodite she sees the female counterpart of her husband Zeus, liberal promiscuity. She has contempt for Aphrodite because of her wounds from Zeus. Aphrodite can teach her to question whether her high ideals of marriage really suit her because Zeus seems to reap all the benefits in terms of freedom, security and sexual independence.

The fractured marriage of Zeus and Hera wasn't always the norm. In ancient times they celebrated the Sacred Marriage. The Earth Goddess and the Sky God renewed the earth with their lovemaking. This ritual copulation was performed in many ancient cultures as a fertility rite. This will be discussed in more detail later in this section as a therapeutic intervention.

Persephone, the Goddess of the Dead, is not someone you would usually notice at first glance in the modern world. Yes, she is attractive and young looking, but her self-effacing attitude may make her appear shy. She is not shy; however, she is just not inclined to assert herself. She is intuitive, vulnerable and yearns for warmth and intimacy.

Due to her psychic nature she usually lives at the borders of reality. The paranormal and metaphysics attract her. She is so secretive and reclusive because she is usually rejected by the mainstream. She needs time to be alone to commune with her unseen spirits. She has a weak ego structure in order to accommodate communication with the spirit world but this makes her susceptible to being overwhelmed by the other side.

As Queen of the Underworld, or the unconscious, all that is repressed is accessible to her. Persephone women today have usually suffered some deep trauma in childhood that plunged them into this archetype. Any trauma during lifetime can cause the Persephone archetype to arise. This traumatic material can cause depression or suicidal tendencies. Hopefully the Persephone who results from a trauma will find a therapist who helps her integrate her experience as an initiation into the realm of death to prepare her for a vocation in some type of psychic work.

To survive Persephone grew up learning to withdraw into herself. This caused a deep alienation that can border on a breakdown at times since she tends to be powerless and have weak ego boundaries. Persephones who can manage their inner worlds tend to become nurses, counselors or metaphysical healers.

Persephone's real issue and wound is with power. She is passive, compliant and powerless. She refuses to own her power and she gives away power. When a woman overidentifies with Persephone she is attracted to situations in which she or others get hurt. She is attracted to men who end up being abusive and she may be accident prone so that she is dependent on others. She is the martyr or the sacrificial victim. What she has failed to understand is that she needs to sacrifice the victim in her to the dark powers, this makes them sacred. All her pain and rage must also be offered up. She could use some of the strength of Athena or freedom of Artemis. She must learn to make commitments and live up to them.

Demeter, the Goddess of Fertility, Motherhood and the Earth, is usually surrounded by children. She can be seen as an inexhaustible supply of energy, changing diapers, making meals and tending sick children. She has an instinctive way of caring for the young. She is dedicated and has that motherly selfless love. She is that fantasy mother that all of us wanted even if we never experienced it, warm, enveloping and utterly satisfying. All the Goddesses can be mothers but for Demeter it is her primary guiding principle almost to the exclusion of everything else.

She lives entirely for her children and is happy and fulfilled being a mother. A young Demeter girl can be recognized playing with dolls or as the older sister who likes to help her mother with the new baby. Artemis would be off playing with boys and Athena would be reading a book. Demeter as a child will be sweet with a loving temperament.

Demeter almost has a symbiotic relationship with her mother. They have the same values and dreams. If the mother does not provide any role modeling for the young Demeter, she will carry her mother and become her mother's mother. She may marry and become pregnant early. The healthy Demeter will seem like a boring homebody to her Goddess sisters who are out dating, winning athletic meets or campaigning for civil rights.

Demeter's sexuality is usually natural and earthy. She does risk being overly attendant on her mate at her own expense. College rarely figures in her plans and she usually marries someone who will stay in same town. Demeter does not marry for position or power like Hera; she is just looking for someone to be a reliable father for her children and who will provide for all of them.

Demeter's fulfillment is in the wonder of her children. Her greatest satisfaction is to see them grow into health, happy adults. But in today's society Demeter has wounds too. Part of Demeter's wound stems from the fact that there is no place in modern society for single mothers. The social system punishes mothers who are not part of the marriage unit.

Another wound is that her birth rights are denied by the mainly male medical profession that interferes with the birthing process. In today's economics mothers must work up until delivery. Childbirth is treated as an emergency instead of a natural process with fetal monitoring, drug-induced labor and caesarian section deliveries. Her sacred functions of childbirth have become mundane and demeaned.

Demeter is prone to victimization and has power and control issues. She does not express anger well. She says yes to everyone to the point that it makes her ill. She fosters dependency in others and can be passive-aggressive. She can also become depressed over an empty nest. To grow she must become her own good mother.

Demeter as the Goddess of the Harvest is also wounded because society today is mostly urban with over 80% of the population living in cities. The old matriarchal ways that were once universal in the peasant communities have been overshadowed by civilization.

Demeter could use the help of Athena to help her fight for mother's rights and Artemis to learn not to be so dependent on a man. Aphrodite could teach her to love someone other than her children. A dialogue with some of her sisters could help to heal some of her wounds.

Every woman has two or three dominant Goddesses in her psyche. She is not likely to completely switch Goddesses at every time of transition in her life but a new phase brings new energies and perspectives, which will be modified by her environment. For example, having a baby will bring you into Demeter's world, going to college will bring you into Athena's world and getting married may bring you into Hera's world.

You can do a journaling exercise to make lists of what you remember about particular times in your life. By viewing this list you can see what the dominant Goddesses have been throughout your life. This will also reveal the Goddesses that have been ignored or avoided. This will suggest the dynamic or the interplay that needs to occur. Whichever Goddess you have unfinished business with is the one who has the least voice or the one who nags at you in the background. This can also be described as your shadow.

Who has the strongest voice? Look at the outside influences that push you or pull you towards one or the other realms of the Goddesses. These outside influences could be your mother, father, community values or occupation. If you are an Athena woman with a Demeter mother you probably feel obligated to have children to please your mother when you would rather be out in the business world or in college. Conversely if you did not receive much mothering as a child part of you may long for that in a child.

Your father's wishes can have tremendous influence on you too. He may have wanted boys and wishes you to be an intellectual Athena so he can have discussions with you or he may have wanted an Artemis with whom he can go fishing or hunting. This can be disastrous for you if you are a Persephone or Demeter. Be authentic, don't mold yourself to meet others expectations.

Lastly what community did you grow up in? Does it value college-bound Athena types, beautiful Aphrodite types or marriageable Heras and Demeters? Your community reflects the average role model that you may have internalized and feel out of sorts if you do not meet those standards.

Different Goddesses are predominant in different parts of your life. Persephone as the Maiden rules childhood and the young girl. Artemis and Athena rule adolescence, young womanhood and the transition. Demeter and Aphrodite rule motherhood, relationships and maturity. Hera rules the second half of life and the woman as an elder. Persephone as the Crone rules old age and death as a wise woman.

One popular game to be played in workshops or circles that is utilized by the Woolgers is called "Everything You Ever Wanted to Know about the Goddess." In this game all the women in the group will sit in a sectioned circle. Each section represents a different Goddess. First they go around the room and someone from each section makes a statement regarding their Goddess, then they will ask questions of the other Goddesses, eventually all will change places and experience a Goddess that is not dominant within them in order to better understand themselves and others.

Not all techniques need be performed in therapy; some can be accomplished on your own or with a group of friends, however deep traumatic issues should be discussed with therapists. Some of the techniques used to get in touch with your Goddesses and resolve issues are journaling, meditation, Goddess games, and discussion with friends.

You can also Aspect the Goddess. This is a creative visualization exercise in which you become the Goddess and see what it feels like to be in her "sandals." What are her issues and what is important to her. Are these also important to you? Some Goddesses just want someone to listen to their complaints, they realize they are not dominant but just want a little understanding. If this Goddess is weak within you and you need her power this is an excellent way to absorb it.

Many Neo-Pagan and Wiccan rituals allow its participants to become the incarnation of the Goddess during their ceremonies. This can be very powerful. It is used to raise energy for magical purposes. It is also very life-affirming for the participants.

In her book, *Celestial Goddesses*, Lisa Hunt (2001) offers a meditative guide for using the Goddesses as archetypes to connect with them on a conscious level through scripted meditations. Meditation accesses the unconscious and brings issues into the conscious. For example her meditation with Artemis explores the wild side of nature and facilitates personal strength. Her meditation with Selene breaks chains of fear that keep you from pursing your dreams. Her meditation with Tara harnesses the inner light and draws power during times of need.

Another great sourcebook for visualizations is *Invoke the Goddess,* by Kala Trobe (2000). She had visualizations of Hindu, Greek and Egyptian deities. The book allows you to channel specific archetypal energies. The deities can be accessed on a personal level as each Goddess has something to offer for your physical, emotional and spiritual life. These encounters make a profound effect on the unconscious and stimulate an innate response for healing and development.

Trobe's visualization of Durga is for strength, Kali is for ending cycles of abuse and overcoming phobias, Laksmi is for wealth, Isis releases powers of intuition, Maat will help with balance decisions, Artemis is for fitness, Persephone is for overcoming regret and depression, Aphrodite is for finding your ideal sexual partner and Iris increases communication skills.

Patricia Lynn Reilly in her book *A God Who Looks Life Me,* (1995) presents methods to help heal spiritual wounds for women who grew up in patriarchal religions. This is a book on personal spirituality that heals religion's far-reaching effects. One of the therapies she suggests is automatic writing in which you write with your nondominant hand as you respond and reflect on issues brought up in the book. She calls for women to reinvent old myths and develop new meditations and rituals.

Myth or story touches the limbic system from a neurological point of view. The limbic system is the emotional center of the brain. The limbic system is where we store all of our past traumas. Any successful therapy creates new stories from the fragments of the old stories but give it an expanded frame of reference with a different emotional valence.

Reilly states that women's only sin is that of self-hatred and self-denigration. The remedy is to practice self-acceptance and self-celebration. She suggests Seven Days of Self-Celebration. She details a seven-day course of visualizations and affirmations to bring about self-acceptance. Reilly also has an excellent exercise to be used for incest survivors in the chapter on Lilith and reclaiming original power.

All in all women are rejecting shame-based religions that were shaped by men and based on men's experiences in favor of a woman-affirming spirituality that recognizes the cultural and religious factors that have influenced a woman's life.

Joan Borysenko in her book *A Woman's Journey to God,* (1999) has suggestions for establishing women's circles. She suggests that the leadership of the circle should rotate so that every woman has the chance to be a facilitator or priestess and choose readings and the theme of the meeting. Second, every woman should have the opportunity to speak uninterrupted from the heart. Third, general conversation waits until the group session is over. For a women's circle to work as both a spiritual and psychological cauldron for growth and change, we must see every woman in the circle as a sister who mirrors back a reflection of ourselves (Bolen, 1994).

When patriarchy suppressed the Mother Goddess it left the lesser Goddesses bitter and wounded. Women as a consequence have had to live alienated from themselves ever since. If we allow them to tell their stories we can bring them together again. Men too are listening to these stories told by their partners, colleagues, mothers, daughters and sisters. This allows them to come to a new understanding also.

<u>Men</u>

Where does Goddess psychology leave men? Men have a difficult time in today's modern world where women are acknowledging their feminine roots and power. As women's roles change so do men's. How do they relate to these awakened women?

The knowledge of archetypal patterns of relating can help modern men get some perspective on what different types of women expect out of their husbands, friends and lovers.

Athena tends to respect only men who have mental muscle, those who are cunning, inventive, daring, practical and creative in crafts. She likes adventurous, competitive men and is stimulated by debate and mental sparring. She is not looking for a family man as she prefers to be single. She will usually be interested in older men or a father figure.

Aphrodite likes her men to look and act strong such as leaders, adventurers and athletes. She admires outgoing, well-traveled men, narcissistic men with strong egos and a healthy amount of self-love. She also likes handsome, sophisticated men with fine tastes and worldliness who treat her to candlelit dinners with soft music and gifts. She likes to dress up and wants to be the Prima Dona to her James Bond man.

Aphrodite's men must be able to perform in bed. Men who fall in love with an Aphrodite woman must be prepared to undergo some pain, hurt, jealousy and rejection.

Persephone wants a spiritual seeker like herself, one who is sympathetic to her ideas and her reality of spiritual influences. She prefers introverts like herself. She has deeply conflicting feelings about men. She loathes conflict and will suppress it if necessary. She has a lack of boundaries and can feel absorbed by her lover if not careful. She can also find herself trapped in a nightmarish relationship of abuse.

Artemis is not usually concerned with men as she loves nature. She tolerates a man if he is similar to her, an achiever or outdoor type who likes physical activity or projects that are physical in nature. She likes emotional distance and undemanding and independent men. She does love beautiful bodies. She loves to dance and is comfortable in her body, to her though dance is for herself, not a ritual that leads to the bedroom (Aphrodite).

Artemis rarely dresses up. She does better with men who are emotionally contained. She wants a sexual partner who is free of all narcissistic needs and demands little of her. A man who is shy and reserved in bed is fine with her as she prefers to initiate sex.

Demeter has endless energy and capacity to love but needs a financial provider. She prefers to be home with the children. The center of her world is home and children. She sees most men as sons. She is not interested in her husband's work as Hera would be. She is your typical "Leave it to Beaver" mom. This kind of relationship can fulfill deep security needs for a man who needs to be mothered.

Hera wants status and power. Her husband must be a provider and someone who is important in the community. She wants ambitious, powerful men who are leaders, executives or politicians. She can be devoted and loyal to one of these men. She wants to share her husband's struggles. She will not tolerate laziness or weakness in a mane. She is one unit with her man.

Men need to recognize the transitions in women's lives to understand them. The woman he married may not be the woman that stands next to him now. Most men will project a lot of Aphrodite onto their mate, which is natural because our society idolizes beauty. They may have married an Aphrodite woman who became Demeter when she had children and is moving towards Hera now that all children have gone.

So as the woman changes into a Demeter type, the man should recognize this and make some changes himself. What she needs now to complement this part of her life is a strong father type. All men have within them heroes, lovers, fathers, leaders, listeners and protectors.

Men can also suppress their feminine side, their anima. They may trade their youth, the importance of love and an appreciation for beauty for their ambitions. They have sacrificed their feminine aspect for power. Their feminine side is not allowed to develop and contribute to the creativity, sensitivity and perspective of the male personality.

When a man is strong in his masculine self, he can begin to acknowledge the feminine within himself. Men have a bigger challenge in this area than women because the Goddesses have been long dormant within them. When the Goddesses awaken in men they are usually projected onto women they are either attracted to or have strong reactions to. They may suddenly develop an interest in children (Demeter), want to dress better (Aphrodite) or discover psychic abilities (Persephone).

As women heal their inner Goddesses we are seeing the birth of tenderness towards men. Once we embrace our own power, we are no longer dependent on men to save us. We can allow men to be human, vulnerable and needy. As we deal with our wounds our partners feel more secure in bringing their own wounds to the surface. They can share their fears and doubts without worrying that we will fall apart or take it personally.

We offer compassion to men. We are now allies in our mutual healing process. Today when we become aware of a problem it is a challenge to be solved together instead of an excuse to blame the other or leave each other.

Sex as Therapy

It is proposed that sex be utilized to heal the wounds between the masculine and the feminine, both on a personal and on a collective basis. This will have profound psychological, spiritual and evolutionary effects. This is the time to reinstitute the "Sacred Marriage", now that the divine feminine is re-emerging into consciousness.

Looking back into ancient history, the Goddesses and Gods were very prolific. Without the intense sexual activity of fertility deities, there could be no productivity in nature. They were not concerned with what they produced because they had to maintain cosmic equilibrium so they were not just entitled, they were duty-bound to produce both good and evil and all variations (Husain, 1997).

The sexuality of the Goddess was prized and respected as it was re-enacted in ritual, emulated by her priestesses and imitated by her followers in orgiastic rituals. The Goddess's sexual life provided a pattern for the system of sacred prostitution in a number of societies where sex was part of the replay of the divine act of creation.

The techniques of sexual pleasure were highly prized by many ancient civilizations that compared it to art or music in modern society. These techniques were practiced and developed to such a level that they became a basis for philosophical and religious thought. In fact the moment of sexual union was thought to be the supreme expression of human creativity.

Ancient civilizations like Sumeria treated sex as a complex and pleasurable activity. It was also considered spiritually and physically beneficial like Yoga. Copulation was defined as an act that was more than mere carnal gratification or for the preservation of the species.

This kind of attitude towards sexuality inspired many erotic texts on the subject formed as religious discourse still in use today. Included in these texts are the Sumerian tablets, Ugaritic ritual dramas, Japanese texts such as Nihongi and some Chinese medical texts. The most famous of these texts is Vatsyayana's *Kama Sutra*, which was written in India between the 3rd and 5th centuries A. D. The notion of sex as a sin is totally absent from these writings.

The *Kama Sutra* is the most famous book on lovemaking ever written. It was originally meant as an instruction book for brides to be. Kama Sutra means "arts of love." It was written by an Indian sage and not translated into English until the 1880s. It was not available to the general reader until the 1960s. Kama is far more than just erotic pleasure; it includes good food, silken clothes, perfumes, music and painting. Sex was considered not only natural but necessary as the human counterpart of creation. The *Kama Sutra* not only had detailed advice on the sexual act itself, including 64 positions but instructions on courtship, marriage, education and household management – what cultured men and women should know to attract the opposite sex. There are also other chapters on prostitutes, courtesans, virgins and the use of go-betweens and harems (Sinha, 1992).

The *Kama Sutra* inspired other sacred texts like the Tantras, which collectively are called Tantrism and date back to the 6th century A.D. Tantrism perceives the universe as a set of energy vibrations emanating from the love-play of the God Shiva and his consort Shakti. One of the five practices of Tantrism is meditations on the art of love. The devotee contemplates desire with the yoni (vulva) of the Goddess as the focus of his worship. Physical intercourse takes place in Tantrism as a mystical union with the Goddess. This union assures peace in the afterlife. Sexual intercourse is believed to open all social barriers and unblock the flow of energies essential to the divine creative function emulated by the devotees in ritual.

This same process can be seen in Wiccan rituals where the God and Goddess are incarnated as the priest and priestess. In Wicca, sexuality is an expression of the creative life force of the universe. It is sacred in the manifestation of the Goddess. It is a sharing of energy in passionate surrender to the Goddess. In orgasm, humans share in the primordial force of the universe (Starhawk, 1999).

At the opposite end of the spectrum are the Christian traditions of the Old Testament that believe fornication is an abomination in filthiness. Women, cities and the Goddess were all condemned as harlots who peddled the filthy commodity of sex, especially Ishtar, referred to as the "Whore of Babylon."

During this time it was customary for many women to live within the temple complex of the Goddess. The temple in earlier times was the heart of the city and owned much of the land and herds. They also kept the cultural and economic records for the city. Women who resided within the temple of the Goddess took lovers from among the community, making love to those who came to the temple to pay honor to the Goddess. Sex was a sacred act so holy that it was performed in the house of the Divine Creatrix. This is thought to have originated from ancient fertility rituals and the relationship of sex to reproduction. In the worship of the Goddess, sex was her gift to humanity (Stone, 1976).

These women, the qadishtu, owned land and other properties and engaged in business activities. They were usually from wealthy families and much sought after as wives. The children born to them inherited their land and names. Women who made love in the temples were referred to as sacred women or the undefiled. The term qadishtu translates as holy women so the term prostitute is not really accurate.

Sacred "prostitution" was a widespread and honorable form of religious worship in ancient civilizations. The terms for these women were devadasi in India and heirodule in Greece. Their names suggest a servant of the divinity. In ancient Mesopotamia, the qadishtu were thought of as servants of the Goddess Ishtar. They would sleep with any worshipper for a fee. The devadasis of India are servants of Jagnnatha and are only supposed to sleep with Brahmin priests at the temple. The sacred prostitute was always the embodiment of the Goddess.

It is believed that this practice originated as a sex act of the Goddess and her son-lover, and was later emulated by her worshippers. Usually the God was played by the high priest or perhaps the king or chief of the land. In this manner a secular ruler received authority directly from the Goddess. This was also a purification ritual.

For some Greek women the profession of hetaera offered a more independent and respected alternative to the subordinate role of wife. They were not prostitutes; they were more like Geishas or courtesans who wielded significant power. They were skilled entertainers and hostesses with educations and cultural interests. Many were leaders in the community.

Deena Metzger in her article titled *Re-Vamping the World: The Return of the Holy Prostitute,* (Zweig, 1990); states that the holy prostitute offered access to the divine as the embodiment of the Goddess. Soldiers returned from war to be cleansed and reunited with their Gods or Goddesses. The sacred prostitute guided men to reconnect with what was holy in them and what was holy in her. Today the consequences of this split in the sacred and the secular are devastating. Now men must face a split projection of the Feminine archetype and seek nurturing from one source and excitement from another.

Metzger calls for a re-vamping of society. She states that we must become sexual-spiritual beings again. We must identify with eros no matter what the seeming consequences. Secondly, we must re-sanctify the body. She states that we must endure the agony of the consciousness required of the heretic. We must commit ourselves to connection when the world values separation. The task is to accept the body as spiritual and sexuality as a spiritual discipline.

The "Sacred Marriage" or hieros gamos was the name of the actual ritual that was performed usually on an annual basis. In the Bronze Age, the sacred marriage of the God and Goddess symbolized the union of the masculine and feminine principles. It was a ceremony to assist in the regeneration of nature.

In Crete the priestess-Queen and the priest-King performed the sacred marriage in costumes. The priestess wore a cow-headed mask and the priest wore a bull-headed mask. The ceremony was performed once every 8 years to renew the King's power. At the end of the ceremony a bull was sacrificed. This probably stems from an earlier ritual in which the Goddess joined with her son-lover and afterwards he was sacrificed to ensure the fertility of the next year. Eventually an animal was substituted.

This ritual was also performed in the temples of Inanna-Ishtar in Sumeria. The King took the role of the bridegroom as her son-lover and the high priestess took the role of the Goddess. Much is written about the sacred marriage of Inanna-Ishtar to Dumuzi-Tammuz. The sacred marriage was not only a fertility rite but it also symbolized the union of the moon and the sun and heaven and earth. It was celebrated in the spring after the God had returned from the Underworld and took place in the bridal chamber at the summit of the temple. What follows are excerpts from the ritual performed that have survived in the form of a poem written by a Sumerian high priestess in 2250 B.C.

(Baring, 1991):

> He brought me into his garden.
> My brother, Dumuzi, brought me into his garden.
> I strolled with him among the standing trees,
> I stood with him among the fallen trees,
> By an apple tree I knelt as is proper.
> Before my brother coming in song,
> Who rose out of the popular leaves,
> Who came to me in the midday heat,
> Before my lord Dumuzi,
> I poured out plants from my womb.
> I placed plants before him,
> I placed grain before him,
> I poured out grain before him.
> I poured out grain from my womb…
>
> Bridegroom, let me caress you,
> My precious caress is more savory than honey,
> In the bedchamber, honey filled,
> Let us enjoy your goodly beauty,
> Lion, let me caress you,
> My precious caress is more savory than honey…
>
> He has sprouted; he has burgeoned;
> He is the lettuce planted by the water.
> He is the one that my womb loves best.
>
> My well-stocked garden of the plain,
> My barley growing high in its furrow,
> My apple tree which bears fruit up to its crown,
> He is lettuce planted by the water.
>
> My honey-man, my honey-man sweetens me always.
> My lord, the honey-man of the gods,
> He is the one that my womb loves best.
> His hand is honey, his foot is honey,
> He sweetens me always…
>
> Now I will caress by high priest on the bed,
> I will caress the faithful shepherd Dumuzi,
> I will caress his loins, the shepherdship of the land,
> I will decree a sweet fate for him.

This poem celebrates the union of man and woman depicting the Gods. It is sexual and sensual in its imagery and shows the tenderness of the relationship and the mutual respect for each other as they ensure the fertility of the land, its people and herds.

The Sacred Marriage between Zeus and Hera was reported to have lasted for 100 years. Hera at one time was a Mother Goddess so it is possible that Zeus was first seen as a son-lover until he acquired all of her power. It is believed that Hera is much older than any of the Olympian Gods. This could be the nature of her constant power struggles with Zeus, a conflict between the older matriarchal and newer patriarchal ways.

With the rise of Judaism, Yahweh had no feminine counterpart, no marriage rites were performed, and no attachment to fertility and the land was seen. Yahweh created from his word. He was not tempered by a feminine quality. In orthodox Christianity the concept of the Sacred Marriage was not possible since Mary was human and Yahweh was divine. However this union was expressed in the Gnostic texts where Mary Magdalene and Jesus loved each other and were possibly married. As stated earlier, the Sacred Marriage was one of the most important rituals in Gnostic Christianity.

In all other cultures, the relationship of the masculine to the feminine as expressed in the Sacred Marriage of Goddess and God always culminated in a religious ritual. This speaks of a universal need to reconcile these two polarities. The divine image must have the ethical word and loving compassion in order to heal and inspire. So it is that the masculine quality of transcendence and the feminine quality of immanence must be present in order for the Sacred Marriage to take place in the soul of humans.

The Sacred Marriage gave the psyche an image of wholeness and relationship. It appears that the psyche needs this image in order to preserve its balance, which depends on an equitable relationship between the masculine and the feminine.

This is what is lost to humanity today. The consciousness is ready to manifest a new, deeper understanding of life's meaning. The joining of the feminine and masculine will give birth to a transformation of the image of deity. This will allow humanity's values to emerge in union.

This union can be accomplished if the Sacred Marriage ritual is returned to its former numinosity. In therapy, couples will be asked to see sex not as sinful or dirty but as a beautiful experience that can be shared; one that will unite them and allow them to experience the divine on a personal level. The role of the therapist will be more of a facilitator, educator or coach.

It should be a mystical experience and should be treated with importance as it was in ancient times, a pleasurable duty. The experience should be surrounded in ritual. First the couple should ground and center themselves into the here and now. They should let go of all worldly concerns and matters and be sure not to be interrupted. Secondly, they should meditate together to relax and enter the same level of calm anticipation. Third, they should bathe together to celebrate each other's body and as a further exercise in harmonizing their energies. The room should be decorated to please all the senses – candles, incense, food and drink, meditative or ritualistic music and clean, soft sheets on the bed or "altar".

There should be no insecurities regarding the body since they are both the incarnation of the spirit of the God and Goddess, the physical shell does not matter. For too long the traditional religions have had a near psychotic rejection of the body. This needs to be overcome, especially for this ritual as the bodies are the vessels of the divine.

Fourth they should have some kind of statement as to what they are about to accomplish to stress the importance of the ritual, a mission purpose as it were or vows as they would be given in a traditional ceremony. The statements should stress mutual respect and affection as well as equality and the end result of the union and its importance personally and universally.

Fifth, now that they understand the importance of this ritual and are on the same energetic and spiritual level of consciousness they can begin to create the new consciousness through their union. It is suggested that they start slowly in order to build their energy levels simultaneously. Once they feel that their energy levels and physical desires are at a peak they may begin intercourse. At climax they should both visualize the merging of the divine feminine and divine masculine.

This merging creates a new consciousness, which melts away their previous animosities for each other and humanity as a whole. When enough couples are joined this way, the synergy it creates will push humanity to its next evolutionary stage, one of union and mutual respect. This respect will carry over into all areas, respect for Mother Nature, respect for other people of other cultures and a planet wide understanding that we are all one.

On a psychological level the Sacred Marriage can also be used for different Goddess archetypes. For example, an Athena woman who is usually rather shy and unconcerned with sex can be healed with different treatment and sexual positions. Since the Athena woman is all about power and control, she might be more comfortable in a position of dominance during sex. Later she may be ready for sex on a more equitable basis.

The Artemis archetype of course will be more comfortable if she initiates sex and her favored positions will be a little wilder and animalistic. Demeter of course is only concerned with the outcome of having children and this ritual promotes a "spiritual" child as an outcome. Hera is traditional so more traditional positions such as the "missionary" may be what appeals to her. The Persephone archetype has oftentimes had some trauma in her life to bring her archetype to the forefront. It will be necessary to discover the nature of her trauma in order to know how to proceed. If the trauma stems from sexual abuse, she may not be ready for this type of ceremony. Once she is ready, it will be important to her to stress the spiritual and metaphysical nature of the ceremony, which will appeal to her. Lastly is the Aphrodite archetype. As the Goddess of love, she will have no problem at all with the ritual and will probably come up with some new ideas as to how to proceed.

Many have expressed concern over the pervasiveness of sex in our society today. The pornographic magazines seem to refute the idea that images advance women's equality. This flood of smut is just another indication that the right hemisphere of the brain is gaining freedom from the left's priggishness. The repression of sex for the last 3000 years has created a longing for release so great that this marked reaction toward the other direction is expected (Shlain, 1998). This will not last. The pendulum will come to rest in the middle. Our culture is relishing in the release of the image and is merely overindulging.

Sex is the life force, the creative power of life. It is an intimate relationship between man and woman and God or Goddess. Women's sexual organs were once honored and revered. Today before we can think of sex as an act of deep communion with the Goddess or God, it has to be reclaimed from the sterile desert of puritanical religion. This may require some healing if we were taught that sex was a nasty necessity of procreation.

CONCLUSIONS

The feminine half of human spirit has been dealt with inadequately by the masculine dominated societies as it evolved in our cultures and civilizations. We see the result of this neglect, which is with us still, in the decay of feeling and caring values and in the pursuit of masculine rationalism, which seems to be the dominant element in the establishments of today. The loss of feminine eventfulness has led to the most urgent and dangerous problem of our time, the exploitation and rejection or our Mother Earth. The feminine must be restored to parity with the masculine in order for humanity to avoid more misery generated by patriarchy – military control, depletion of the earth's resources and disregard of other cultures. The return of the Goddess entails a harmonious sharing of power that benefits everyone.

This is not a return of the old form of the Goddess because we have evolved and she has evolved along with us. This is a return of the Goddess values that will fit into our society and make them whole again. The historical sacrifice of the Goddess principle is recognized on some level as necessary for the evolutionary development of the technological gains of patriarchy and the development of separate, individual egos. But the Goddess principles have been absent too long and are needed now to temper the masculine principles, which have proceeded too long alone.

We must not fail the challenge to transcend our opposites in something that will combine to balance both the masculine and the feminine and in their union, create something greater than the sum of their parts (Baring, 1993).

The Goddess is waiting for us to remember her so that we may heal ourselves and the world. We can bring her back by understanding the Goddess archetypes and their dynamics. We may then take the next step to a divine union by participating in the Sacred Marriage of masculine and feminine, not only physically but spiritually and psychologically.

FUTURE OF THE GODDESS AND HUMANITY

Harvey believes that humanity has 20 years at most if we do not make changes, and that was 13 years ago (Harvey 1995). Unless we awaken to the mystery of the sacred feminine and allow it to illuminate every area of our lives and to create in it harmony, justice, peace, love, ecstasy and balance we will die out and take nature or a large part of it with us. Regarding the powers of destruction that ravage nature, we must make changes "the human race has no hope of survival unless it chooses to undergo a total transformation, a total change of heart" (Harvey 1995). What is required is a massive and unprecedented spiritual transformation or we die out.

Harvey espouses a Goddess revolution to dissolve all dogmas and hierarchies without exception. The revolution of the Mother demands of each of us unstinting service. Service means dedicating our every gift and power, our every prayer, our every thought and emotion and perception to the welfare of others in the world. The Son will come back when the Mother is present (Harvey, 1995).

As stated before, evolution is not predetermined, we are active co-creators of our present and future so we can make choices that benefit everyone. It is never too late to start. Individual development proceeds only by means of affiliation and cooperation between the masculine and the feminine.

Bibliography

Adler, Margot. *Drawing Down the Moon, Witches, Druids, Goddess-Worshippers and Other Pagans in America Today.* New York, New York: Penguin Group, 1986.

Avila, Elena. *Woman Who Glows in the Dark.* New York, New York: Penguin Putnam Books, 1999.

Baring, Anne and Cashford, Jules. *The Myth of the Goddess, Evolution of an Image.* New York, New York: Penguin Books, 1993.

Bennett, James and Crowley, Vivianne. *Magic and Mysteries of Ancient Egypt.* New York, New York: Sterling Publishing Company, 2001.

Bess, Savitri. *The Path of the Mother.* New York, New York: Ballantine Publishing Group, 2000.

Bolen, Jean Shinoda. *Crossing To Avalon.* San Francisco, Ca: Harper Collins Publishers, 1994.

Bolen, Jean Shinoda. *Goddesses in Every Woman.* New York: One Spirit, 1984.

Bolen, Jean Shinoda. *Gods in Every Man.* New York: One Spirit, 1989.

Borysenko, Joan. *A Woman's Journey to God.* New York, New York: Riverhead Books, 1999.

Bulfinch, Thomas. *Bulfinch's Mythology, The Age of Fable.* Crawfordsville, IN: R.R. Donnelley & Sons Company, 1968.

Cotterell, Arthur and Storm, Rachel. *The Ultimate Encyclopedia of Mythology.* New York: Lorenz Books, 1999.

Dee, Jonathan. *Isis, Queen of Egyptian Magic.* New York, New York: Sterling Publishing Co, Inc., 2000.

Eisler, Riane. *The Chalice and the Blade.* San Francisco, Ca: Harper Collins Publishers, 1988.

Estes, Clarissa Pinkola. *Women Who Run with the Wolves, Myths and Stories of the Wild Woman Archetype.* New York, New York: Ballantine Books, 1995.

Gimbutas, Marija and Marler, John (ed.). *The Civilization of the Goddess.* San Francisco: Harper, 1991.

Gonzalez-Wippler, Migene. *Rituals and Spells of Santeria.* New York, New York, Original Publications, 1984.

Graves, Robert. *The White Goddess, a Historical Grammary of Poetic Myth.* New York, New York: Farrar, Strauss and Giroux, 1975.

Harvey, Andrew. *The Return of the Mother.* New York, New York: Penguin Putnam, Inc., 1995.

Hunt, Lisa. *Celestial Goddesses.* St. Paul: Llewellyn Publications, 2001.

Husain, Shahrukh. *The Goddess.* Alexandria,Va: Time-Life Books, 1997.

Jordan, Michael. *Encyclopedia of Gods.* New York, New York: Facts on File, Inc., 1993.

Kraemer, Ross Shepard. *Women's Religions in the Greco-Roman World.* Oxford: University Press, 2004.

Lerner, Harriet Goldhor. *Women in Therapy.* New York, New York: Harper and Row Publishers, 1988.

Markale, Jean. *The Great Goddess.* Rochester, Vermont: Inner Tradtions, 1997.

Neumann, Erich. *The Great Mother, An Analysis of the Archetype.* Princeton, N.J.: Princeton University Press, 1974.

Pattanaik, Devdutt. *The Goddess in India, The Five Faces of the Eternal Feminine.* Rochester, Vermont: Inner Traditions, 2000.

Reilly, Patricia. *A God Who Looks Like Me, Discovering a Woman-Affirming Spirituality.* New York, New York: Ballantine Books, 1995.

Rothberg, Donald and Kelly, Sean, eds. *Ken Wilber in Dialogue, Conversations with Leading Transpersonal Thinkers.* Wheaton, Illinois: Quest Books, 1998.

Schlain, Leonard. *Sex, Time and Power, How Women's Sexuality Shaped Human Evolution.* New York, New York: Viking Books, 2003.

Shlain, Leonard. *The Alphabet Versus the Goddess, The Conflict Between Word and Image.* New York, New York: Penguin Group, 1998.

Sinha, Indra, translator. *Kama Sutra.* London: Harper Collins Books, 1992.

Starhawk. *The Spiral Dance, A Rebirth of the Ancient Religion of the Great Goddess.* San Francisco, Ca: Harper Collins Publishers, 1999.

Stone, Merlin. *When God was a Woman, The Landmark Exploration of the Ancient Worship of the Great Goddess and the Eventual Suppression of Women's Rites.* New York, New York: Harcourt Brace & Company, 1976.

Trobe, Kala. *Invoke the Goddess, Visualizations of Hindu, Greek and Egyptian Deities.* St Paul, Minnesota: Llewellyn Publications, 2000.

Turabian, Kate. *A Manual for Writers.* Chicago: University of Chicago Press, 1996.

Vega, Marta Moreno. *The Altar of my Soul.* New York, New York: Ballantine Publishing Group, 2000.

Ventura, Varla. *Sheroes.* Berkley, Ca: Conari Press, 1998.

Woolger, Roger and Jennifer. *The Goddess Within, A Guide to the Eternal Myths that Shape Women's Lives.* New York, New York: Ballantine Books, 1989.

Zweig, Connie, Ed. *To Be Woman, The Birth of the Conscious Feminine.* Los Angeles, Ca.: Jeremy Tarcher, Inc., 1990.

Appendix A

A Correlational Study of the Keirsey Temperament

Sorter and Selected God/Goddess Archetypes

INTRODUCTION

There is a specific need in psychotherapy today to sometimes make quick assessments of personality in order to decide how to proceed with a client. In some therapeutic settings, such as brief therapy or pastoral counseling it would be considered too invasive to administer lengthy personality tests. Assessments must be developed that would allow the counselor to make quick personality judgments without disrupting the rapport that has been established. This quick assessment must also be presented in terms that are familiar and interesting to the client.

A possible solution to this problem would be asking the client to view a list of God/Goddess archetypes or role models. The client would then be asked to select one that she feels relates to her. Her selection will provide insight as to her personality and current issues. This test would be relatively noninvasive and can be administered in a few minutes.

If answering truthfully and without bias, the client should be able to select the archetype which matches her actual personality type. Then to prove this hypothesis, that clients can actually select their personality type, a personality test will be administered to subjects in addition to God/Goddess profiles. The personality test selected is the Keirsey

Temperament Sorter. Statistical analysis should prove that there is a correlation between specific archetypes and specific personality categories.

Unfortunately, significant associations were not found, but other interesting results were obtained which will be reported in the results section. Reasons for the inability of the subjects to choose the correct archetype are also discussed later in this paper.

History of Temperament and Keirsey

Temperament is similar to personality in many ways, but it is actually a part of personality. Temperament is one's innate abilities, one's potential characteristics, weaknesses and strengths. This is of course influenced by your environment. Temperament plus environment equals personality (Keirsey, 1998).

Temperament theory proposes that people have an intact temperament at birth. They are predisposed to behave in particular and predictable manners. Temperament theory has a long history in one form or another. The Roman physician Galen in 190 A.D., building on previous theory of Hippocrates in 370 B.C., postulated that a balance of bodily fluids, called "humors" determined our actions. Prior to that time, personality was thought to be influenced by the stars or the Gods. The four humors were blood, black bile, yellow bile and phlegm. If the blood dominates the other humors then we are called Sanguine. Those of Sanguine temperament are very optimistic. If the black bile is dominant in our system then we are Melancholic in temperament. If the yellow bile is strongest then we are considered Choleric or passionate. If the phlegm is strongest them we are called Phlegmatic or calm (Keirsey, 1978).

Plato wrote in "The Republic" about four kinds of characters which resemble these four humors. Of course Plato was more concerned with social roles. He called the Sanguine temperament, the "iconic" which translates to the Artisan temperament that Keirsey utilizes. The Melancholic temperament, he called the "pistic" which is now seen as Keirsey's Guardian temperament. The Choleric temperament was called the "noetic" by Plato and is now called the Idealist by Keirsey. And lastly the Phlegmatic was called the "dianoetic" seen today as the Rational.

Aristotle had a different theory from his mentor Plato. Aristotle regarded happiness as being important and defining character. He proposed that there are four types of happiness: sensual pleasure or "hedone" (Artisan), a pleasure in acquiring assets called "propraietari" (Guardian), the pleasure of moral virtue or "ethikos" (Idealist) and lastly the pleasure derived from logic or "dialogike" (Rational).

In a somewhat similar vein, a 16th century physician, Paracelsus believed that four totem spirits characterized humans. These four spirits are "Salamanders", who are impulsive (Artisans), the "Gnomes", who are hard-working (Guardians), the "Nymphs", who are passionate (Idealists) and the "Slyphs", who are calm (Rationals).

Not all physicians of the time agreed with the humors theory but it was very popular among the playwrights like Shakespeare who made many references to the humors in his plays. Novelists such as Austen, Tolstoy and D.H. Lawrence also utilized the four types of characters in their books.

In the early field of psychology, temperament was almost extinguished by Freud and Pavlov who believed man was a creature of instinct until social field theory was introduced in Europe. In 1905 Adickes divided humans into four "world-views" –

Innovative, Traditional, Doctrinaire and Skeptical. In 1914 Spranger stated that four

attitudes – Artistic, Economic, Religious and Theoretic determine personality. And in

1920, Kretschmer believed that there were four characters – Hypomanic, Depressive,

Hyperesthetic and Anesthetic. In 1947 Rudolph Dreikurs proposed four goals to boost

self-esteem: Retaliation, Service, Recognition and Power. Finally in 1947 Eric Fromm

believed that four orientations represented personality: Exploitative, Hoarding, Receptive

and Marketing (Keirsey, 1998).

    All of these theorists looked at temperament and personality from different points

of view; however, they still had similar conclusions. This seems to indicate a trend for

over 2000 years regarding temperament and its usefulness.

    The Keirsey Temperament Sorter owes much of its development to Carl Jung and

Isabel Myers. In the 1920's Carl Jung claimed in his book, *Psychological Types* that

people had many instincts – archetypes that are driven internally with none being more

superior over the others. He claimed the importance of extraversion and introversion and

described four psychological functions – "thinking", "feeling", "sensation" and

"intuition". He proposed that most humans show a marked preference for one type and

we can be identified by this type (Jung, 1923).

    In the mid-1950s, Isabel Myers and her mother Kathryn Briggs devised a

questionnaire based on Jung's theories which would identify different types of

personalities. This was called the Myers-Briggs Type Indicator. It identified 16

personality patterns of action and attitude. This test became very popular and is still in

use today (Myers, 1962).

    Myers labeled her personality types with letters chosen from four pairs. They are:

E – Extraverted	or	I – Introverted
S – Sensory	or	N – Intuitive
T- Thinking	or	F – Feeling
J – Judging	or	P – Perceiving

By extraverted, Myers meant the person was outgoing. Introverts are more reserved. Sensory people are observant of their surroundings, while Intuitive types are introspective. Thinking types are objective, while Feeling types are sympathetic. Finally, Judging types like to make and keep schedules, while Perceiving types are always looking for alternatives. Your type will have four of these letters, for example ESTJ. The sixteen combinations can be grouped into four similar groups:

SPs (Artisans) - ESTP, ISTP, ESFP, ISFP
SJs (Guardians) - ESTJ, ISTJ, ESFJ, ISFJ
NFs (Idealists) - ENFJ, INFJ, ENFP, INFP
NTs (Rationals) - ENTJ, INTJ, ENTP, INTP

Myers believed that all types differed and excelled in different areas. There are no good and bad temperaments, some perform better in certain situations. The social context determines the most effective personality.

In describing the four groups of personalities, Myers stated that the SPs (Keirsey's Artisans) are continuously probing their environment to detect options that are favorable to them. They are exciting and impulsive and everything they do is practical and effective. They often enjoy life, are artistic and athletic and can be gifted with tools.

The SJs (Guardians) are similar to the SPs in that they are observant of their surroundings but because they like to schedule their own and everyone else's activities. Myers has described them as conservative, reutilized, dependable, hardworking and persevering.

The NFs (Idealists) are the opposites of the SPs. The NFs are introspective, friendly and try to give meaning to people's lives. They want everyone to feel good about themselves. Myers has described them as sympathetic, religious, creative and subjective.

The NTs (Rationals) are also introspective. They are the opposite of the SJs. They can be tough-minded in figuring out technology to solve problems. They are persistent and rational in all actions. Myers has described them as analytical, abstract, intellectual, curious and independent.

Keirsey believes that there are 2 basic dimensions of personality: 1) how we communicate and 2) how we use tools to accomplish our goals. Communication can be abstract (NFs and NTs) or concrete (SPs and SJs). Tool usage can be cooperative (SJs and NFs) or utilitarian (NTs and SPs). Cooperators will attempt to attain their goals by getting along with others while utilitarians will use the most effective way possible.

Where Keirsey differentiates his theory from Myers is that he believes that it is more effective to base the personality types on observable actions as opposed to thought processes. Myers based her theory on psychological functions. Since it can be difficult to determine what someone is thinking, Keirsey calls his system based on intelligent roles, what people do well and their skilled actions which are more observable (Keirsey, 1998).

Keirsey believes that the personality is already whole at birth and merely differentiates into the mature being it is meant to be, like an acorn into an oak tree. It emerges as an individual (Keirsey, 1998).

Current and Past Research

Despite some differences in theory, the Myers-Briggs Type Indicator (MBTI) and the Keirsey Temperament Sorter II (KTS) seem to be measuring the same constructs and seem to obtain the same results. Irving Tucker found that in a study of the two tests and Keirsey's computer based test that all three tests were measuring equally (Tucker, 1993). Quinn tested 191 university students and found that the results support the use of either instrument to determine personality type (Quinn, 1992). Kelly reported in a study of the two tests that there were moderate to strong positive correlations (Kelly, 2001).

Other contemporary studies utilizing the KTS showed interesting results in different areas. For example, Waskel examined the intensity of and the ability to identify a midlife crisis in 331 subjects. He found that five temperaments thought more about death – ESTJ, ISTJ, ESFJ, ISFJ and ENFP (Waskel, 1995). Most of these fall under the Guardian category, which are known for worrying. Swanger found in a study that examined personality types and profitability as a restaurant manager that 69% of the managers in the high profit range tested as ESTJ (Swanger, 1998). ESTJs are the Guardian Supervisors and would be perfect in that role. Mccann found when testing 75 therapists that more intuitive than sensing types were in the therapist population (Mccann, 1998). This also makes sense as all Idealists are intuitive and many would excel as counselors. Fearn found in a study of attitudes toward Christianity that out of 367 religion students, the ideal type among students was the ENFJ (Fearn, 2001), which is an Idealist, known for religious attitudes.

METHOD

As noted above, the KTS was the selected personality test to be administered to the subjects. Testing materials were ordered from the Keirsey website (www.keirsey.com) at a minimal cost. The tests can be self-scored but for consistency the author scored them. Over 200 packets were assembled. These testing packets consisted of an informational sheet that contained a release for subject's signature; a KTS test and a God/Goddess Archetype Sheet (see Appendix, figure 1 for a copy of the Archetype Sheet with the correct answers in parentheses).

The God/Goddess Archetype Sheet was developed utilizing four Gods – Dionysus, Zeus, Hermes and Apollo and four Goddesses – Artemis, Demeter, Aphrodite and Athena. Descriptions of each archetype followed. Subjects were asked to select the archetype that most resembled them. Descriptions of archetypes were obtained from various literatures on mythology (Bolen, 1984 & 1989, Bulfinch, 1968, Cotterell & Storm, 1999, Hunt, 2001, Jordan, 1993). The Greek pantheon was selected since it is most familiar to the public. Included in the description of each archetype were descriptors obtained from Keirsey on his four groups of personality. For example, Dionysus's description contained information on his background according to mythology and descriptive words used by Keirsey to define the group Artisans. Archetypes were matched up to the personality which closely resembled them. Some were directly referred to by Keirsey (Keirsey, 1998). The following is a summary of these:

Dionysus – Artisan   Artemis – Artisan
Zeus – Guardian   Demeter – Guardian
Hermes – Idealist   Aphrodite – Idealist
Apollo – Rational   Athena – Rational

There were a total of 156 subjects. The majority of the subjects (82) were obtained from a local Religious Science Church, herein after called "the Church Group." The Church Group has very liberal beliefs. They also have a large neo-pagan or earth-based religion membership. This church would be familiar and receptive to God/Goddess archetypes. The second largest group of subjects (48) was law enforcement agents in a

Federal agency, a very conservative group. This provided contrast to the first group of subjects. The third and last group of subjects was called other (26) and was comprised of a group of nurses and friends and relatives of subjects in other groups.

Figure 1. Subjects

Church Group-CG	82	52.6 %
Law Enforcement	48	30.8 %
Other	26	16.7 %
Total	156	100 %

For the Church Group subjects (CG), announcements were made in the church newsletter soliciting subjects. Packets were left in a box in the Great Hall. Subjects picked up the packets and filled them out then returned them to the box for collection. Law Enforcement subjects (LE) were solicited in person and Other (O) subjects heard by word of mouth.

Data was gathered from November 2003 until February 2004. In February 2004 a workshop was held at the Church Group Center. Approximately half of the total number of subjects was present to receive a 10 page analysis of their personality type. This analysis included information on mating and dating, careers and parenting – all derived from Keirsey's books (Keirsey, 1978 & 1998). A PowerPoint presentation was given explaining all the personality groups. The LE and O group's results of those that were not present at the workshop were returned electronically.

RESULTS

This was a simple correlational, cross-sectional design. All measures were taken at one time. This design was selected due to its simplicity and ease of administration and because it was useful in determining if the two variables were related. The independent variable was the population of subjects. There was no random assignment of subjects as they fell into predetermined categories. The dependent variables were the results of the two tests or the group to which subjects were assigned due to their answers on the Keirsey and their ability to guess their proper archetype on the God/Goddess archetype test.

The data was nominal with a dichotomous population so the binomial nonparametric test of significance was utilized. The null hypothesis was that there would be no relationship between the two tests and the alternate hypothesis was that there would be a relationship between the two tests or that the subjects would be able to guess their correct archetype, thereby affirming the use of the simpler, noninvasive test.

In Figure 2 below we see the total number of subjects and that no data was missing.

Figure 2 General Statistics

		gender	subject group	Pop w/three groups	temperament	God archetype	God/type match
N	Valid	156	156	156	156	156	156
	Missing	0	0	0	0	0	0

In Figure 3 below indicates the gender breakdown. Of the 156 subjects, 90 were female and 66 were male.

Figure 3. Gender

		Frequency	Percent	Valid Percent	Cumulative Percent
Valid	female	90	57.7	57.7	57.7
	male	66	42.3	42.3	100.0
	Total	156	100.0	100.0	

In Figure 4 below, we see the frequency of the results of the KTS. Of the 156 subjects, 10 or 6.4% were Artisans. This is interesting since according to Keirsey, approximately 30-35% of the general population are Artisans. There were 88 Guardians or 56%. In the general population, there is 40-45%. There were a total of 52 or 33.3% of the subjects were Idealists, which in the general population is only 15%. And in this study there were 6 Rationals or 3.8%. In the general population there are 10% (Keirsey, 1998).

Figure 4, Temperament Group (Keirsey)

		Frequency	Percent	Valid Percent	Cumulative Percent
Valid	Artisan	10	6.4	6.4	6.4
	Guardian	88	56.4	56.4	62.8
	Idealist	52	33.3	33.3	96.2
	Rational	6	3.8	3.8	100.0
	Total	156	100.0	100.0	

In Figure 5 we see the answers to the Archetype test. The most common Goddess selected was Aphrodite and the most commonly selected God was Apollo.

Figure 5 God Archetype Selected

		Frequency	Percent	Valid Percent	Cumulative Percent
Valid	Aphrodite, Idealist	40	25.6	25.6	25.6
	Apollo, Rational	24	15.4	15.4	41.0
	Artemis, Artisan	12	7.7	7.7	48.7
	Athena, Rational	15	9.6	9.6	58.3
	Demeter, Guardian	12	7.7	7.7	66.0
	Dionysus, Artisan	13	8.3	8.3	74.4
	Hermes, Idealist	27	17.3	17.3	91.7
	Zeus, Guardian	13	8.3	8.3	100.0
	Total	156	100.0	100.0	

Figure 6 below indicates that most of the subjects, 60.9% could not select the archetype that matched their personality.

Figure 6 God/type match

		Frequency	Percent	Valid Percent	Cumulative Percent
Valid	no	95	60.9	60.9	60.9
	yes	61	39.1	39.1	100.0
	Total	156	100.0	100.0	

In Figure 7 we see the results of the nonparametric binomial test for significance. Group 1 could not guess the correct archetype for their personality type and Group 2 was able to make the correct choice. According to these results, the null hypothesis cannot be rejected, so there is no significant relationship between the two tests. They do not appear to measure the same constructs.

Figure 7 Binomial Test

		Category	N	Observed Prop.	Test Prop.	Asymp. Sig. (2-tailed)
Numeric God Match	Group 1	.00	95	.61	.50	.008
	Group 2	1.00	61	.39		
	Total		156	1.00		

(Based on Z Approximation)

Before discussing the implications of the results, let us examine some cross tabulations of the data to see what patterns emerge than can help explain the results. Appendix B is a cross tabulation of the subjects' temperament based on the KTS results and if the selected archetype was a match or not. It is interesting to note that 100% of the Artisans and 75% of the Guardians could not select their proper archetype. However, 67% of the Idealists and 66% of the Rationals could. This would make sense as both Idealists and Rationals are more introspective than the Artisans and Guardians. What Gods did they select?

Figure 8 Cross tabulation of Temperament, God Selected Comb & Gender

	God Selected		Total

gender		AF-HE, Idealist	AR-DI, Artisan	AT-AP, Rational	DE-ZE, Guardian	
female temperament	Artisan	5				5
	Guardian	19	5	11	11	46
	Idealist	22	9	4	2	37
	Rational			2		2
Total		46	14	17	13	90
male temperament	Artisan	3		2		5
	Guardian	6	8	18	10	42
	Idealist	12	3			15
	Rational			2	2	4
Total		21	11	22	12	66

Figure 8 shows a cross tabulation of God selected by temperament and separated out for gender. Both female and male Artisans seemed to incorrectly prefer the Idealist archetype. Female Guardians seem to prefer Aphrodite instead of Demeter, the correct Goddess. Male Guardians seemed to prefer Apollo instead of Zeus, the correct archetype. Both male and female Idealists seemed to correctly prefer the Aphrodite/Hermes archetype. Also both male and female Rationals correctly prefer the Apollo/Athena. The majority of females selected Aphrodite and the males seemed to be split among Hermes and Apollo. This seems to indicate there may be some problems with the descriptions of the Gods or most subjects selected who they would like to be as opposed to who they really are.

What differences can be found among the subject groups? Appendix C demonstrates that the group of subjects from the Church Group was the best at selecting their correct archetype. Approximately 55% could not guess correctly and 45% did guess correctly. This is higher than the 39% overall. The Church Group is characteristically more introspective than the Law Enforcement or Other group. Of the Law Enforcement group, 73% were unable to select their correct archetype. The Other group was behind the Church Group in that, 42% guessed correctly. Half of the Other group was from the

Nursing profession. Health care providers may also be more introspective by nature of their employment.

DISCUSSION

As noted above there is no correlation between the two tests – the Keirsey Temperament Sorter II and the God/Goddess Archetype. They do not measure the same construct. More work needs to be completed on the definitions of the Gods and Goddesses so that they more closely resemble the four temperament categories. This may be a validity problem that needs to be overcome before it can be further tested. The Archetype test also needs better reliability. A few subjects mistakenly filled out the test twice. Although the Keirsey showed the same results, the Archetype test did not.

One factor may be better control of the test-taking environment. Ideally it would have been best for all tests to be administered at once with the same oral and verbal instructions given. Instead the tests were taken home and completed. Subjects may have shared their tests which could have resulted in Hawthorne effects. Also experimenter effects could have interfered with the results. The subjects may have skewed their results knowing that the experimenter would score them, trying to make an impression on the experimenter.

If these validity and reliability factors can be overcome, the God/Goddess Archetype Test could become an instrument to be utilized in brief therapy especially with clients who are more introspective, those who are members of earth-based religions and those who are familiar with archetypes as role models.

Bibliography

Barron, Renee. *What Type Am I?* New York, New York: Penguin Books, 1998.

Bolen, Jean Shinoda. *Goddesses in Every Woman.* New York: One Spirit, 1984.

Bolen, Jean Shinoda. *Gods in Every Man.* New York: One Spirit, 1989.

Booth, Wayne, Colomb, Gregory and Williams, Joseph. *The Craft of Research.* Chicago: The University of Chicago Press, 1995.

Bulfinch, Thomas. *Bulfinch's Mythology, The Age of Fable.* Crawfordsville, IN: R.R. Donnelley & Sons Company, 1968.

Cohen, Jacob. *Statistical Power Analysis for the Behavioral Sciences.* New Jersey: Lawrence Elrbaum Associates, Publishers, 1988.

Cotterell, Arthur and Storm, Rachel. *The Ultimate Encyclopedia of Mythology.* New York: Lorenz Books, 1999.

Fearn, Mike, "Attitude toward Christianity and Psychological Type: A Survey among Religious Studies Students," *Pastoral Psychology,* Vol 49(5) (May 2001): 341-348.

Gonick, Larry and Smith, Woollcott. *The Cartoon Guide to Statistics.* New York, New York: HarperCollins, 1993.

Hunt, Lisa. *Celestial Goddesses.* St. Paul: Llewellyn Publications, 2001.

Jordan, Michael. *Encyclopedia of Gods.* New York, New York: Facts on File, Inc., 1993.

Jung, Carl. *Psychological Types.* New York: Harcourt Brace, 1923.

Keirsey, David and Bates, Marilyn. *Please Understand Me.* Del Mar, CA: Prometheus Nemesis Book Company, 1978.

Keirsey, David. *Videotape: Please Understand Me.* Del Mar, CA: Prometheus Nemesis Book Company, 1995.

Keirsey, David. *Please Understand Me II.* Del Mar, CA: Prometheus Nemesis Book Company, 1998.

Kelly, Kevin, "Concurrent Validity of the Online Version of Keirsey Temperament Sorter II," *Journal of Career Assessment,* Vol. 9(1) (Win 2001): 49-59.

Mccann, Geneva, "The Selection of Therapeutic Mechanisms of Change in Relation to Therapist Temperament," *Dissertation Abstracts International,* Vol. 58(11-B) (May 1998): 6240.

Montgomery, Stephen. *People Patterns.* Del Mar, CA: Archer Publications, 2002.

Myers, Isabel. *Manual: The Myers-Briggs Type Indicator.* Palo Alto, California: Consulting Psychologists Press, 1962.

Quinn, Michael, "A Cross-Correlation of the Myers-Briggs and Keirsey Instruments," *Journal of College Student Development,* Vol. 33(3) (May 1992): 279-280.

Runyon, Richard and Haber, Audrey. *Fundamentals of Behavioral Statistics.* New York: McGraw-Hill, 1991.

Sheskin, David. *Handbook of Parametric and Nonparametric Statistical Procedures.* New York: CRC Press, 1997.

Spector, Paul. *Research Design.* Newbury Park, CA: Sage Publications, 1981.

Swanger, Nancy, "Quick Service Chain Restaurant Managers: Temperament and Profitability," *Dissertation Abstracts International,* Vol. 59(3) (Sep 1998): 693.

Tieger, Paul and Barbara Barron-Tieger, *Do What You Are.* New York: Little, Brown and Company, 2001.

Tucker, Irving, "Correlations among Three Measures of Personality Type," *Perceptual and Motor Skills,* Vol. 77(2) (Oct 1993): 650.

Turabian, Kate. *A Manual for Writers.* Chicago: University of Chicago Press, 1996.

Waskel, Shirley, "Temperament Types: Midlife Death Concerns, Demographics and Intensity of Crisis," *Journal of Psychology,* Vol. 129(2) (Mar 1995): 221-233.

Appendix B

Goddess Wheel Questionnaire
By Roger and Jennifer Woolger, 1989

Read the following six statements in each section. Next rate how much or how little each statement applies to you and circle an appropriate number. (For men, simply assess how much or how little the six statements apply to the woman or type of woman you are most drawn to.) Then circle the appropriate number. There is a self-scoring answer key at the end to help you determine your Goddess profile.

Rating Key

3 = Strongly applies
2 = Moderately applies
1 = Mildly applies
-1 = Not true at all

QUESTIONNAIRE

ONE: **Appearance** (*How I look/ How she looks*)

A Since I don't go out a lot, clothes and makeup
   aren't that important to me.   3 2 1 -1
B I much prefer to be dressed in jeans and
   comfortable shirts.   3 2 1 -1
C My appearance is rather unconventional.   3 2 1 -1
D I like to be well, but conservatively dressed and
   use makeup sparingly.   3 2 1 -1
E I love to make myself up and be attractive.   3 2 1 -1
F Being well dressed and made up gives me
   confidence to go out into the world.   3 2 1 -1

TWO: **My Body** (*How I feel about it/ How she feels about it*)

A I tend not to think much about my body.   3 2 1 -1
B My body feels best when I'm fit and active.   3 2 1 -1
C I like my body to be touched a lot by those I
   love.   3 2 1 -1
D I'm often not in my body at all.   3 2 1 -1
E I find it embarrassing to talk about my body.   3 2 1 -1
F I love being pregnant / I look forward to being
   pregnant.   3 2 1 -1

THREE: **House and Home** (*What matters to me / What matters to her*)

A I much prefer my home to be elegant and impressive.   3 2 1 -1
B I much prefer the city; an apartment is fine.   3 2 1 -1
C My home must be warm and have room for   3 2 1 -1
D I need privacy and space for the things I like to do.   3 2 1 -1
E Wherever I live must be comfortable and beautiful.   3 2 1 -1
F I prefer to live in the country or where I am
      close to parks and open spaces.   3 2 1 -1

FOUR: **Eating and Food** (*Its importance to me / Its importance to her*)

A I eat carefully to keep my body healthy.   3 2 1 -1
B I like to dine somewhere romantic.   3 2 1 -1
C I like to eat out a lot and be able to talk.   3 2 1 -1
D I really enjoy cooking for others.   3 2 1 -1
E Mealtimes are important family occasions.   3 2 1 -1
F Eating isn't terribly important to me.   3 2 1 -1

FIVE: **Childhood** (*How I used to be / How she used to be*)

A I had lots of secret games and imaginary worlds.   3 2 1 -1
B I always ran all the games with my friends.   3 2 1 -1
C I mostly loved to play with dolls.   3 2 1 -1
D I always had my nose in a book as I got older.   3 2 1 -1
E I loved to be outdoors and with animals.   3 2 1 -1
F I loved changing clothes and playing dress-up.   3 2 1 -1

SIX: **Men** (*What I need in one / What she needs in one*)

A I want a man who will always excite me sexually.   3 2 1 -1
B I want a man to protect and spoil me.   3 2 1 -1
C I like a man who is independent and gives a lot of space.   3 2 1 -1
D I need a man who will challenge me mentally.   3 2 1 -1
E I need a man to understand my inner world.   3 2 1 -1
F I want a man whose position in the world I can be proud of. 3 2 1 -1

SEVEN: **Love and Marriage** (*What they mean to me/ What they mean to her*)

A Marriage only works when there is a higher spiritual connection. 3 2 1 -1
B Marriage is the foundation of society.   3 2 1 -1
C Love is all-important; without it my marriage is empty.   3 2 1 -1
D Love and marriage are fine so long as I have freedom.   3 2 1 -1
E Marriage safeguards my children; love alone is not enough.   3 2 1 -1
F My marriage sometimes has to be sacrificed for the sake of my work. 3 2 1 -1

EIGHT: **Sexuality** (*How I am in bed / How she is in bed*)

A It's sometimes hard to let myself go fully during sex.   3 2 1 -1
B I get turned on very easily by the right man.   3 2 1 -1
C It sometimes takes me a while to get into my body.   3 2 1 -1
D I love to give sexually as much as to receive.   3 2 1 -1
E I'm a bit shy, but I can be very wild.   3 2 1 -1
F Sex can be ecstatic and almost mystical for me.   3 2 1 -1

NINE: **Children** (*Their role in my life / Their role in her life*)
(If you don't have children imagine what it would be like)

A I'm happier when doing things outdoors with my kids.   3 2 1 -1
B My children are the greatest fulfillment of my life.   3 2 1 -1
C I expect my children to be a great credit to me.   3 2 1 -1
D I choose not to have children so that I can pursue my career.   3 2 1 -1
E I love my kids, but my love life is equally important.   3 2 1 -1
F I love my children and always want to know what they're feeling
    and thinking.   3 2 1 -1

TEN: **Pastimes** (*Types of things I like to do / Types of things she likes to do*)

A Metaphysics, tarot reading, astrology, dream journal, New Age
    workshops, personal art and rituals.   3 2 1 -1
B Collecting jewelry, art objects, beautiful clothes; fashion, music,
    theater.   3 2 1 -1
C Sports, athletics, jogging, camping, fishing, sailing, horseback riding.   3 2 1 -1
D Community involvement, social clubs, volunteer groups, local church.   3 2 1 -1
E Political campaigning, minority group support, museums, lecture series,
    reading.   3 2 1 -1
F Cooking, baking, gardening, tending plants, needlework, weaving.   3 2 1 -1

ELEVEN: **Parties** (*How I am at them / How she is at them*)

A I usually get into political or intellectual discussions.   3 2 1 -1
B I'm often drawn to people with problems.   3 2 1 -1
C I much prefer to be the hostess at my own party.   3 2 1 -1
D I can't help sizing up the sexiest men in the room.   3 2 1 -1
E I like to make sure that people have a good time.   3 2 1 -1
F Parties make me restless so I don't go to too many.   3 2 1 -1

TWELVE: **Friends** (*Their place in my life / Their place in her life*)

A Most of my friends have children the same age as mine.   3 2 1 -1
B I choose my friends carefully and they are very important to me.   3 2 1 -1
C I enjoy my latest ideas and projects with both my women and men

friends.   3 2 1 -1

D I tend to have magical friendships.   3 2 1 -1
E My friends are mostly the wives of my husband's friends.   3 2 1 -1
F My men friends are generally more important to me than my
women friends.   3 2 1 -1

THIRTEEN: **Books** *(What I mostly have around / What she mostly has around)*

A Cookbooks, craftbooks, child care books.   3 2 1 -1
B Serious nonfiction, biographies, coffee table books,
travel books, illustrated history.   3 2 1 -1
C New Age books, psychology, metaphysics, channeled books, I Ching. 3 2 1 -1
D Sports, fitness, and yoga manuals, animal books, wildlife books,
how-to books.   3 2 1 -1
E Art books, popular biographies, novels, romances, poetry.   3 2 1 -1
F Politics, sociology, recent intellectual books, avant-garde
literature, feminist books.   3 2 1 -1

FOURTEEN: **The Large World** *(My attitude toward it / Her attitude toward it)*

A I always try to stay informed about what's going on in the world.   3 2 1 -1
B Politics only interest me for the intrigues behind the scenes.   3 2 1 -1
C I know more about the world from my dreams than from the news-
paper or TV.   3 2 1 -1
D I rarely know what's going on – or care!   3 2 1 -1
E It's mostly a man's world, so I leave them to it.   3 2 1 -1
F It's important for me to play an active role in the community.   3 2 1 -1

Goddess Rating Sheet

Go through the questionnaire, redistributing each of your six ratings for each section among the six Goddess columns. You will find the six letters, A-F, arranged under the name of the Goddess they belong to. Simply enter the scores and add up each Goddess column. Goddesses that you are strong in will naturally be high scores, while undeveloped or disowned Goddesses will be low or minus scores. This is your Goddess profile.

Athena	Aphrodite	Persephone	Artemis	Demeter	Hera
1=F__	1=E__	1=C__	1=B__	1=A__	1=D__
2=A__	2=C__	2=D__	2=B__	2=F__	2=E__
3=B__	3=E__	3=D__	3=F__	3=C__	3=A__
4=C__	4=B__	4=F__	4=A__	4=D__	4=E__
5=D__	5=F__	5=A__	5=E__	5=C__	5=B__
6=D__	6=A__	6=E__	6=C__	6=B__	6=F__
7=F__	7=C__	7=A__	7=D__	7=E__	7=B__
8=C__	8=B__	8=F__	8=E__	8=D__	8=A__
9=D__	9=E__	9=F__	9=A__	9=B__	9=C__
10=E__	10=B__	10=A__	10=C__	10=F__	10=D__
11=A__	10=D__	11=B__	11=F__	11=E__	11=C__
12=C__	12=F__	12=D__	12=B__	12=A__	12=E__
13=F__	13=E__	13=C__	13=D__	13=A__	13=B__
14=A__	14=B__	14=C__	14=D__	14=E__	14=F__

TOTALS

___   ___   ___   ___   ___   ___

Appendix C

The Goddess Wheel

CPSIA information can be obtained at www.ICGtesting.com
Printed in the USA
BVOW09s1007210915

418919BV00020B/502/P